nem̲ ̲ ̲ ̲ ̲poole

Katy Perry

Katy Perry

California Gurl

JO BERRY

Copyright © Orion 2011

This edition first published in Great Britain in 2011 by
Orion Books
an imprint of the Orion Publishing Group Ltd
Orion House, 5 Upper St Martin's Lane,
London WC2H 9EA
An Hachette UK Company

1 3 5 7 9 10 8 6 4 2

A CIP catalogue record for this book is available
from the British Library.

ISBN: 978 1 409 1 33612

Printed in Great Britain by CPI Mackays, Chatham ME5 8TD

The Orion Publishing Group's policy is to use papers that are natural,
renewable and recyclable and made from wood grown in sustainable
forests. The logging and manufacturing processes are expected to
conform to the environmental regulations of the country of origin.

Every effort has been made to fulfil requirements with regard to
reproducing copyright material. The author and publisher will be
glad to rectify any omissions at the earliest opportunity.

www.orionbooks.co.uk

Contents

List of Illustrations

Katy Perry attends the Katy Perry Concert at Fritzclub at the Postbahnhof on September 17, 2008 in Berlin, Germany. (Photo by Florian Seefried/Getty Images)

Katy Perry poses with the award for Best International Female Solo Artist backstage during the Brit Awards 2009 at Earls Court on February 18, 2009 in London, England. (Photo by Eamonn McCormack/WireImage)

Katy Perry poses with a gold disc prior to her own concert at Fritzclub at the Postbahnhof on September 17, 2008 in Berlin, Germany. (Photo by Florian Seefried/Getty Images)

Katy Perry arrives at the 51st Annual Grammy Awards held at the Staples Center on February 8, 2009 in Los Angeles, California. (Photo by Larry Busacca/Getty Images)

Katy Perry arrives for the MTV Europe Music Awards, held at the Echo Arena on November 6, 2008 in Liverpool, England. (Photo by Getty Images)

Katy Perry performs at 102.7 KIIS FM's Jingle Ball 2010 at

Nokia Theatre L.A. Live on December 5, 2010 in Los Angeles, California. (Getty Images)

Katy Perry performs onstage during 'VH1 Divas Salute the Troops' presented by the USO at the MCAS Miramar on December 3, 2010 in Miramar, California. 'VH1 Divas Salute the Troops' concert event will be televised on Sunday, December 5 at 9:00 PM ET/PT on VH1. (Photo by Michael Caulfield/Getty Images for VH1)

Katy Perry arrives for the MTV Europe Music Awards, held at the Echo Arena on November 6, 2008 in Liverpool, England. (Photo by Getty Images)

Musicians Travis McCoy and Katy Perry at the 2008 MTV Video Music Awards at Paramount Pictures Studios on September 7, 2008 in Los Angeles, California. (Photo by Chris Polk/FilmMagic)

Katy Perry and Rihanna attend Karl Lagerfeld Pret a Porter show as part of the Paris Womenswear Fashion Week Spring/Summer 2010 Jardin des Tuileries on October 4, 2009 in Paris, France. (Photo by Eric Ryan/Getty Images)

Katy Perry aka Katy Brand accepts the Favorite Female Artist and Favorite Online Sensation awards onstage during the 2011 People's Choice Awards at Nokia Theatre L.A. Live on January 5, 2011 in Los Angeles, California. (Photo by Kevin Winter/Getty Images)

Katy Perry and Russell Brand attend the 52nd Annual GRAMMY Awards held at Staples Center on January 31, 2010 in Los Angeles, California. (Getty Images)

Katy Perry and actor/comedian Russell Brand attend The Art of Elysium's 3rd Annual Black Tie Charity Gala 'Heaven' on January 16, 2010 in Beverly Hills, California. (Photo by Donato Sardella/WireImage)

Katy Perry performs during the ski winter opening on November 28, 2009 in Ischgl, Austria. (Photo by Goran Gajanin/Getty Images)

Katy Perry attends the 'Life Ball 2009 at the city hall on May 16, 2009 in Vienna, Austria. (Photo by Florian Seefried/Getty Images)

Katy Perry attends Z100's Jingle Ball 2010 presented by H&M at Madison Square Garden on December 10, 2010 in New York City. (Photo by Kevin Mazur/WireImage for Clear Channel)

Katy Perry performs at 102.7 KIIS FM's Jingle Ball 2010 at Nokia Theatre L.A. Live on December 5, 2010 in Los Angeles, California. (Getty Images)

Katy Perry onstage at the MTV Europe Music Awards, held at the Echo Arena on November 6, 2008 in Liverpool, England. (Photo by Getty Images/Getty Images)

Katy Perry performs during the 2009 MTV Europe Music Awards held at the O2 Arena on November 5, 2009 in Berlin, Germany. (Photo by Dave M. Benett/Getty Images)

Katy Perry onstage at the MTV Europe Music Awards, held at the Echo Arena on November 6, 2008 in Liverpool, England. (Photo by Getty Images)

Katy Perry hosting the MTV Europe Music Awards for the second year running. The show was broadcast live from Berlin on MTV on 5 November. (Photo by Dave Hogan/Getty Images)

Singer Katy Perry performs onstage during 'VH1 Divas Salute the Troops' presented by the USO at the MCAS Miramar on December 3, 2010 in Miramar, California. (Getty Images)

1
In the Beginning . . .

Today's pop stars are often created. Our TV schedules are packed with reality shows promising to deliver the next singing sensation, only for many of them to fade away after their first album flops, perhaps popping up a couple of years later in a local panto. While shows like *Popstars*, *The X Factor* and *American Idol* have given us the occasional super-star (Cheryl Cole, Leona Lewis, Kelly Clarkson and Jennifer Hudson being the cream of the reality crop from both sides of the Atlantic), the true, talented artists are more likely the ones who weren't discovered overnight, manufactured and repackaged to fit the current fashion, but the ones who have worked hard, paid their dues in grimy clubs, pubs and bars with beer-stained floors, and fought for their career every step of the way on their own terms.

Katy Perry is one such talent. She wasn't discovered by Simon Cowell, and her rise to pop stardom didn't happen overnight, either. While her high-waisted shorts, Fifties-style make-up and eyebrow-raising corset tops are a stylist's dream, like Madonna in the Eighties embracing lace and crucifixes, Katy created her own image, developed her own

1

style, and wrote her own songs, so that we fans know that the Katy we see on stage and on TV is the real one, not some music executive's idea of what a pop star should be.

Her beginnings, however, were decidedly un-pop-star-like. Katy didn't perform in local talent competitions like Cheryl Cole did, she didn't spend her pre-teen years with Mickey Mouse like Justin Timberlake and Britney Spears, and she didn't begin auditioning for acting and singing roles when she was ten like Kylie Minogue. Although her family had a background in the entertainment industry – her uncle was Frank Perry, the director of the movie *Mommie Dearest*, that cult kitsch classic starring Faye Dunaway as movie-mother-from-hell Joan Crawford, and her aunt was a screen-writer – Katy's origins were less starry and it was a while before the bright lights of Los Angeles beckoned.

Raised by parents who were 'Evangelical, with a heavy Pentecostal flavour' pastors, fair-haired baby Katheryn Elizabeth Hudson (Katy later changed her surname to Perry to avoid confusion with actress Kate Hudson) was born on 25 October 1984 in Santa Barbara.

A pretty, historic coastal town in California, Santa Barbara was perfect for growing up in. Part of an area described as the American Riviera, it is just over ninety miles north of Los Angeles, and is a haven for movie stars wanting to escape the madness of Hollywood. Nestled in Santa Barbara County, the town is framed by the Santa Ynez mountains and boasts beautiful beaches, the Los Padres national forest, and vine-yards that litter the valleys, all within exploring distance. It also has its own zoo, which Katy visited as a child with her family, a botanical garden, marine park and Mission Santa

Barbara, well known as one of the most beautiful buildings in California. Originally built in 1786 (therefore ancient by American standards!), it was destroyed by an earthquake in 1812, but has been rebuilt and is still a functioning, and very pretty, Catholic church. Known as Queen of the Missions, it – and the surrounding countryside – probably looks familiar even if you have never been to California, as Santa Barbara has been the home to numerous film and TV productions including the comedy *Sideways*, the Keanu Reeves drama *A Walk in the Clouds*, *L.A. Story*, *The Graduate* and, of course, the late-Eighties daytime soap *Santa Barbara*.

In these lovely surroundings, Katy, the middle child of three – she has an older sister, Angela, born in 1982, and younger brother, David, born in 1987 – didn't grow up dreaming of being a pop star – mainly because she didn't know what one was! While other young kids were listening to rap and watching MTV, little Katy was being raised in a strict Christian household where no pop music, no MTV and no boys were allowed. Instead the radio was tuned to Christian stations and Katy's first experience of live music was seeing the choir at church.

'I didn't know there was a New Kids on the Block out there because the people that I surrounded myself with had the same upbringing [as me],' she told Sheryl Garratt in the *Observer* newspaper. 'It was all gospel and Christian music.'

Rock music wasn't the only thing banned in the Hudson household, as Katy told *Cosmopolitan* magazine. 'I was banned from reading *Cosmo* because there was too much sex! I'm sure my parents didn't *not* want me to know about sex, but they didn't want me to have a tutorial! And there was always someone on the cover with cleavage. It turned out all right, though – I've posed for *Cosmo* with my cleavage out! There you go, mum! It all worked!'

In fact, Katy's strict childhood is most reminiscent of another sexy female pop star, Madonna. She too had grown up in a religious household, raised a Catholic by her mother (who died when Madonna was five) and father, and she was also another middle child who used music – and the occasional rebellious act – to distinguish herself from her siblings. As girls, they both explored their musical side – Katy singing, Madonna dancing – and as adults, the two women have become known for their unique styles, their ability to amuse, to entertain and, of course, to shock.

For Madonna this has meant appearing nude in a book she published entitled *Sex*, posing with a crown of thorns on her head at Easter, releasing videos known for their raunch (such as 'Like a Prayer', packed with religious imagery that shocked the Christian community, and the steamy 'Erotica'), and, of course, distinguishing herself in the early years by wearing lacy corsets draped with crucifixes, pearls and chains, plus a belt with a buckle that said 'Boy Toy'. The Catholic girl even managed to outrage the Pope himself, by rolling around on stage to her hit 'Like a Virgin' during the 1990 Blond Ambition tour, causing his holiness to ask devout Christians to boycott the concerts.

Of course, Katy was only five years old and had her hair in bunches when Madonna was at her most controversial, and no doubt little Katy Hudson was unaware for another decade that such scandalous things went on outside her Christian community. But it is interesting to note the similarities between the two performers now – religious upbringings, a tough time getting to the top, their sexy styles and unique ways of grabbing headlines. For while Katy may not have offended the Vatican, in her short career she has raised many an eyebrow for her song lyrics, videos, clothes and cheeky manner in interviews. And Madonna herself may have noticed the similarities – just as Katy's career was beginning to take off, Madonna mentioned this talented young girl from Santa Barbara in a handful of interviews, commenting that Katy's song 'Ur So Gay' was her favourite song of the moment, and thus giving Katy a welcome boost to her public profile.

It seems, not surprisingly, that Madonna knew a pop superstar when she saw one. (The pair finally met in 2008, with Katy telling the *Sun* that she was ' . . . so nervous. I got so weak in the knees and I thought I was going to throw up. But I needn't have worried. She was cool. She was so petite. She comes up to my chest and I thought she was supposed to be a giant!')

Back in the late Eighties and early Nineties, however, Katy's home life certainly didn't seem like one where a future pop star and favourite of Madonna would be made. She was only allowed to go roller-skating at the local Santa Barbara rink on Tuesday nights as that was when it was Christian night. Rock music was considered by her parents to be the devil's work and TV channels such as MTV were banned, although Katy and her siblings figured out the pass-code they needed to get the cable TV working when their parents were out so that they could secretly tune in. And Katy was only allowed to bring home friends if they were Christians.

'We spoke in tongues,' she remembered when being interviewed for *Blender* magazine. 'We knew there was this one way, and all the other ways were wrong.' Even devilled eggs were called angel eggs in her house. 'I didn't know enough to ask my mom, "How come we call them that? Everybody else calls them something else!"'

Katy wasn't naïve, however, and while she may not have been able to read teenage magazines in the house, she got her information elsewhere. 'At around twelve, I started to get curious about sex,' remembers the girl who is now known for her sexy image and cupcake bra. 'I had a friend at fifteen who was more cultured than me – smarter, cooler, well-travelled, so I learned stuff from her. She was great, and showed me good music and introduced me to things like sushi.'

Before her career took off, Katy told local journalist Mike Rimmer that she was religiously devoted as a child: 'I was one of those kids going to [religious summer] camp and every time there was an altar call I was there.' (An altar call is when a member of the congregation comes forward to make a spiritual commitment to Jesus.) It certainly meant an interesting upbringing for the young girl – the family travelled around America when Katy was little, so her father Keith, who describes himself as a 'prophet/evangelist', could spread the word and, he believes, use his religious power to heal people he met along the way.

As Katy and her siblings grew up, Keith ran his own ministry on the road, which continues to this day. Keith Hudson Ministries are, according to his website (www.keithhudson. org), there to help understand divine encounters and the anointing. 'We have crossed a new threshold in the time line of God and many believers have risen with an unquenchable hunger to know their God and do great exploits,' Keith says. 'These new believers are after the kingdom of power and glory. Divine encounters have become the norm for many and others are finding that what God has done for others in this new move He is doing for them.'

'Divine encounters are quickly maturing many in the body of Christ through fresh revelation resulting in the release of incredible displays of supernatural ability marked with signs and wonders by the Holy Spirit,' he adds. On the website Keith explains that he is used by the Lord to expose and dispel spiritual lethargy, with the help of wife Mary, from their base in Oceanside, California (a growing city near San Diego that boasts Legoland as one of its attractions). Both of them have written books on the subject, too. Keith's book, *The Cry*, is a prayer resource book, while Mary's book *Smart Bombs* apparently 'reveals how the word of God is like a modern-day smart bomb'.

The ministry is now a much larger business than it was when Katy was growing up. Back then, it operated out of small buildings and churches mainly in California, whereas now, Keith and Mary often travel across Europe and the USA to spread the word. In recent years they have preached in France, Belgium, Singapore, Malaysia, Hawaii, Italy and Germany – their 'tours' almost rivalling Katy's musical ones!

It was, not surprisingly, their California church congregation who first heard Katy's pretty singing voice back in 1993. She started singing in the Oasis Christian Center at the age of nine, and carried on until she was sixteen – partly thanks to the influence of her sister. Katy admits she copied everything that her big sister Angela did, so when Angela asked for singing lessons, Katy decided she wanted them too.

It wasn't until Katy was eleven that the family finally stopped travelling and made Santa Barbara their permanent home, moving to a series of houses before settling into a pretty home on a suburban street called Mountain Avenue. By then, she was a bit of a tomboy, often returning home 'bashed and bruised' from playing outside, and already displaying the talent to shock that she has become known for as an adult. 'I was a hyperactive kid and my mom and dad got used to me creating a stir,' she told journalist Adrian Thrills. 'Whether we were on holiday or eating around the dining table, I would always come up with something outrageous.'

It was once they were firmly based in Santa Barbara that other people began to notice Katy's talent. The former assistant pastor of the church, Manny Earnst, remembers her well. 'Music was part of her life ever since I met her; in fact, we had a nickname for her, "Katy Bird", because every time I came into the house she was singing.'

'Katy got her first guitar through the church,' recalls Katy's youth pastor, Jeremy Kraus. 'We got this guitar and gave it to her on her thirteenth birthday. She was just so stoked to have her own guitar and she was on that thing twenty-four-seven.' She spent a lot of time at home in her room, playing the guitar they gave her. 'It was in this house [on Mountain Avenue] where I wrote my first song, which was called "Trust in Me",' Katy remembers. 'It ended up going on the gospel album I recorded when I was fifteen. All the songs I wrote [at that time] were related to my faith and the questions I sometimes had about it.'

Katy didn't dream of being a star with her singing, though. As she told the TV show *MTV Hoods*, 'I never really dreamed about being famous because there wasn't a whole lot of that famous/pop culture idea going on in the house. I knew that Gwen Stefani existed, and Madonna. In fact, Madonna was super-taboo – we didn't even *talk* about Madonna in my household!'

Despite her strict surroundings, or perhaps because of them, her quirky style began to shine through even before she reached her teens. 'When I was eleven or twelve, I had the coolest fake-leopard-print coat. I went to school wearing this coat and everyone made fun of me. But I was proved right at the end of the day, because when all the mothers came to pick up the kids, they loved it. I sold it to the second-hand shop two years later to get more clothes. I wish I'd kept it, but a girl has to have something else to wear!'

Her fashion style was the first sign of a rebellion against her upbringing. As well as falling in love with the style of Nabokov heroine *Lolita*, as portrayed by Dominique Swain in the 1997 film adaptation ('I was like, I wanna wear little jumpers! And rompers! And look like a pin-up!'), Katy wasn't behaving too well at school or at home during her early teens, either. She started skipping school and drinking, and it was after one Sunday morning hangover that she finally learned a secret her parents had been keeping from her.

Concerned about his daughter's drinking, Keith Hudson sat down and told her about his own wild days, her mother's, and their conversion to a better life. While Katy and her siblings had always believed her parents spent their entire life before children on the straight and narrow, her dad soon revealed that was not the case.

Katy's mum, Mary Perry, was a young woman who had grown up in the luscious coastal surroundings of Southern California, a pretty debutante of German and Portuguese descent. She had run off against her own parents' wishes to see the world, however, and ended up married and living in Zimbabwe, before divorcing and returning to the USA where she met Katy's dad. If that wasn't enough to make a young choir singer's jaw drop, there were more revelations to come. As well as her mother also confessing to a relationship with Jimi Hendrix when he was living in Spain ('He just came up to her in a club and picked her up,' Katy later revealed in an interview), Katy's dad Keith had a few surprises of his own.

It seems that he was a scenester on the West Coast of America in the 1960s – basically a guy who followed a rock band across the country like a groupie – and he was also a dealer of LSD (specialising in a potent version called Strawberry Fields) who counted renowned psychedelic drug exponent Timothy Leary as a good friend. '[My parents] found God at a time when they really needed to,' Katy told *Blender* magazine, 'and I believe in the God they found. My dad would have died from one tab of Strawberry Fields too many if he hadn't found God.'

Her parents' revelations may have shocked her, because Katy quietened down a little at school and, during her freshman year at Dos Pueblos High School, she joined the school choir. It wasn't her first time performing in front of people – she had auditioned for a local production of *Fiddler on the*

Roof at the Santa Barbara High School Theater when she was twelve. 'I was an extra in *Fiddler on the Roof*,' Katy laughs, 'because no one knew my talent back then! I wasn't really nervous performing, I was always really excited to be on stage in any capacity – even if I was a guy with a moustache in *Fiddler*!'

The production's director remembers Katy well. 'She was extremely talented and fearless and undaunted by convention,' says Monique Mitchell. 'She's an original.' Despite thinking this, Monique didn't increase Katy's part. 'I was a little bit envious of other people's bigger parts, as I was just a male bystander and I had one little solo and that was it. No lead, nothing!' laughs Katy.

While she may have been in the background, being in the production did spark Katy's love of make-up and showmanship. When *MTV Hoods* took her back to the theatre she had performed in, she wandered backstage to where the cast had applied their make-up. 'I think this is where I first got interested in doing heavy make-up and colour on my eyes and painting my lips, and basically making myself look like a bona fide geisha!'

MTV Hoods also had a surprise for Katy when she visited the theatre – they brought along a handsome man who had appeared on stage in *Fiddler on the Roof* with Katy . . . and also stolen her heart off stage!

The pair's reunion on camera was fun, with Katy admitting that their relationship lasted for only 'a hot second'. He then revealed she had been his first kiss, causing Katy to blush. And there were more red-faced moments to come when a couple of love letters she had written were produced:

'After *Fiddler on the Roof* was done, I remember you went on some summertime trip and you sent me letters.'

Aww, young love. But it wasn't to be – Katy went off to summer camp and met another boy. 'That was interesting,' Katy told the MTV cameras. 'I can't believe I was such a little slut, writing love letters at that age!'

Just a year later, Katy moved from the small, local schools she was used to, to the massive complex that is Dos Pueblos High School, where she spent her freshman year (aged fourteen). Just fifteen minutes away from her house, in the town of Goleta, the school teaches more than 2,300 children and is a National Blue Ribbon School, meaning it has received the highest honour it can achieve for success in teaching. Boasting its own theatre, jazz choir and concert band, it was the perfect place for Katy to learn more about performance and singing. She's not the only musical former pupil, either (though perhaps the most famous) – both guitarist Ryan Mendez (of the band Yellowcard) and blues singer Kim Wilson, the lead singer for the Fabulous Thunderbirds, also attended the school.

By this time, Katy had dyed her hair, changing the natural light brown colour to a more dramatic black, and at Dos Pueblos she came out of her shell and was known for being a class joker and entertainer. 'It was my first real taste of public school,' Katy told *MTV Hoods* when she returned to the site of her teenage years. 'I was discovering all these things I hadn't been exposed to before.' Amongst the huge, red concrete buildings that make up the school, she laughed and joked with her friends while on her way to lessons. 'She's always been really outgoing, really loud, and she doesn't ever get embarrassed – no matter how embarrassed she should be!' remembers childhood pal Becky Curry.

Other friends happily reminisced with *MTV Hoods* about school days with Katy. One friend told the cameras: 'You kind of loved her and hated her at the same time because she was so strange and so weird. You either got her, or you didn't.'

Katy clearly loved the school, because in 2010 she contacted the staff at Dos Pueblos to ask whether she could give a free concert to the students. On Tuesday, 14 September, Katy performed to over 2,000 of them – after having apparently been advised by senior staff members that they would prefer her performance to be 'school appropriate'. They also scheduled it after classes were finished for the day so that anyone offended by her racy stage persona could leave if they wanted to! Speaking from the stage, Katy said to the crowd: 'Maybe you don't know, but I went to high school here. I was on this very stage many a lunch-time. I was such a show-off. There was a pumpkin pie-eating contest, and I won!'

Her visit brought back a lot of memories of her school days – especially when Katy spotted her high-school crush in the crowd. In between songs, Katy called out 'You were the most popular kid in my class! But you never wanted to date me. Oh yeah, you really chose right, honey,' she laughed. 'What's up now, player? I'm going to dedicate this next one to [you]!' Katy then embarrassed the former football quarterback by singing 'Ur So Gay', which features lyrics such as 'You walk around like you're oh so debonair / You pull 'em down and there's really nothing there . . . ' Poor guy!

School friends remembered Katy performing in the

school 'quad' that she revisited in 2010 – a large outdoor area where kids sat to have their lunch. Often, there would be impromptu singing competitions amongst the students, and Katy even decided to perform when it was a free-styling contest one lunch-time – instead of singing she would be expected to rap something off the top of her head. It didn't go too well for her, as up in front of all the kids she realised she couldn't do off-the-cuff rhyming. For possibly the only time in her career, Katy was booed off stage, as fellow pupils chanted 'You can't rhyme!' 'That was one of the saddest days of my life,' she recalled when she returned to the school as an adult.

She wasn't deterred. Instead, Katy remembers, 'I walked the halls, being late to classes of course, really preoccupied with thoughts of being a musician or making a record. That's all I wanted to do.'

When she wasn't at school, Katy would head to Santa Barbara's East Beach to think about how she would achieve her dream. Sometimes she would skateboard ('I was kind of alright at it', she once said, though she teased one journalist by pretending she used to skateboard in heels) or surf with the other kids ('Whenever I was cold I would piss myself in the wetsuit to get warm – all surfers do that!'), but she would mainly think about writing music and singing. And despite being groomed to be lead vocalist in the school choir, and with another three years of high school ahead of her, it was here that Katy made a very important decision.

She decided to drop out of high school and pursue her dream of becoming a singer-songwriter. The bright lights of country music mecca Nashville beckoned, but Katy wasn't to know that a singing career wouldn't happen overnight. For her, it would take a lot of work over seven long years, a lot of disappointment, *and* a drastic change in musical style before her dream would come true ...

2

Katy Hudson

As country and western fans know, if you want to make it in C&W, Christian or gospel music, the city of Nashville in Tennessee is the place to be, and it was here that a young Katy Hudson decided to make her first steps on the road to a musical career.

A large city with a subtropical climate (it's hot and humid in summer, mild in winter), Nashville is home to more than 600,000 people. By 1925 it had already become known as Music City USA, due to the Grand Ole Opry, a country music concert stage that has welcomed performers of bluegrass, folk, country and gospel music to its weekly performances. Musical legends Hank Williams, Patsy Cline, Dolly Parton, Garth Brooks and *American Idol* winner Carrie Underwood have all performed there, often with the concerts broadcast on TV and radio.

They also all often call into the city's Country Music Hall of Fame and Museum, a stunning curved building with long windows that make it look like a piano keyboard, a tower with round discs symbolising the different sizes of vinyl and CD that country music has been recorded on, and an overall shape that, if viewed from the air, looks like the bass clef musical symbol.

Everywhere you look in Nashville, there is evidence that it is a musical town, a sure-fire draw for fifteen-year-old Katy. The city is home to the Tennessee Performing Arts Center, the Nashville Opera, the Nashville Ballet and the Belcourt Theater, while if you wander through downtown Nashville you will find lots of honky-tonk bars around 'the District' (near Lower Broadway and Second Avenue).

The city also has its own 'Music Row' – the home of hundreds of businesses related to country, gospel and contemporary Christian music. This is where record labels such as RCA (in whose Studio B Elvis Presley first recorded) are based, along with music publishing and licensing houses and radio stations. Near the centre of this musical hub, there's a park dedicated to songwriter and performer Owen Bradley, considered to be one of the chief exponents of Nashville's unique sound in the 1950s and '60s, and around his statue (of him playing a piano) you can often find a young busker singing to the passers-by.

Katy, however, didn't have to sing on the street. After her freshman year at school in Santa Barbara, she took her GED (the equivalent of a high-school diploma), and then, while singing in the local choir, she gained a manager, Clifford Scamara, who tried to book her into as many live performances as he could. 'I got her into the biggest Christian festivals around,' he says. 'Even though she was young she was very driven, and she seemed to have a lot of fun on stage.'

It was after seeing her perform that Katy was approached by a couple of Nashville music executives who invited her to come and record some demo Christian music records for them. With her parents' permission, Katy headed off for the city and nervously walked into the first recording studio she had ever been into, to make her first album. It must have been an exciting and also scary time – working with experienced producers and musicians, finally getting to record her voice so that others could hear what a talent she was, but also being away from home for the first time in an imposing city brimming over with musical history.

'I started going to Nashville to record some gospel songs, and to be around amazing country-music vets and learn how to craft a song and play guitar,' she remembered to MTV. 'I'd actually have to super-glue the tips of my fingers because they hurt so much from playing guitar all day, you know? And from that, I made the best record I could make as a gospel singer at fifteen.'

Christian pop and gospel music is certainly a massive industry in the USA. Artists such as Amy Grant and Avalon sell albums in their millions, and the genre even has its own music charts – *Billboard* magazine's Top Christian Albums and Hot Christian Songs list – while many acts 'cross over' into mainstream music charts, too.

Katy just wanted to make a record that showed her religious feelings and her thoughts about life as a Christian teenager, and she just hoped others would like the music she made. She was signed to Red Hill Records, a pop/youth music subdivision of a Christian music label called Pamplin Music that began in 1995. Soon, instead of attending school like her friends back in Santa Barbara, Katy was spending her days in the record label's studio, recording the tracks along

with an acoustic guitar player and a handful of rock musicians. The album that followed, *Katy Hudson* (the album
cover featuring a close-up of Katy's face, her hair once again
blonde) was released in 2001 just as Katy was about to turn
sixteen.

A Christian pop album, it features songs including 'Trust
in Me', written by Katy, 'When There's Nothing Left', 'My
Own Monster' and the trance-y 'Faith Won't Fail'. Each has
distinctive lyrics, as we have come to expect from pop queen
Katy, whether on the chorus of 'Piercing' ('You're piercing
me / This self will bleed / You're killing all of my securities /
Lord, help me see the reality / That all I'll ever need is You')
or during coming-of-age song 'Growing Pains' ('You would
think that I could find a simple song / a photograph of mine
/ To show this public eye / what I have to offer / I may not
have a PHD / or speak in eloquent philosophy! / I'm nothing
more than simply me you see!')

A few journalists got to hear Katy's album in 2001 before
it was released, with Tony Cummings of Cross Rhythms
(Christian Radio Online) writing the following in his review
of her debut: 'Katy clearly is a real vocal talent and the breath-
taking fact that she's a mere sixteen years old suggests a
major star in the making. The production/arrangements by
Tommy Collier, Otto Price and David Browning are exem-
plary and the songs, whether dealing with the challenges of
moving into adulthood both physical and spiritual ('Growing
Pains') or a bold declaration of the reliability of trust in Christ
('Faith Don't Fail'), are top notch. All but the most cynical of
fans should investigate this bright new talent.'

Praise indeed. Unfortunately, Tony Cummings was one

of only a few people to hear the album (if you're very lucky, a copy occasionally pops up on Amazon or eBay, but it's rare). Only a few hundred copies of the Katy Hudson CD were made as, unbeknownst to Katy, Red Hill and parent company Pamplin were on the brink of collapse.

'It [the CD] was sold out of the back seat of someone's car, practically,' Katy joked to reporter Sheryl Garratt seven years later, when the wound was no longer fresh in Katy's heart. 'Just after the record came out, the label went bankrupt. I'm not ashamed of it – everyone's [now] looking for me to be "Well, I'm so ashamed of it and that's why 'I kissed a girl'!" No way! I still have "Jesus" tattooed on my wrist. And I still have a faith and foundation of my own.'

It was that faith, in God and in her own talent, which kept Katy going. While many teenagers, faced with a failed record, would have headed home and given up, Katy picked herself up and carried on. 'She was very determined to be what she wanted to become,' remembers Katy's assistant pastor, Manny Earnst, 'so she made some sacrifices. For a girl of fifteen or sixteen years old, that's a hard decision.'

Jeremy Kraus, Katy's youth pastor, also remembers that time in Katy's career very well. 'Unfortunately her record never got [properly] released, the company went under and the CDs that weren't released were put in the dumpster,' he says. 'Unfortunately that was Katy's humble beginnings with a record label.'

The future looked uncertain. 'I didn't know what to do after the whole Christian music thing didn't work out,' Katy remembers. 'I thought maybe I needed to learn even more about how to write a song so I ended up taking a class about it.' Back home in Santa Barbara, she decided to learn every-thing she possibly could, enlisting fellow class members to teach her piano and guitar while she worked out what to do next. The problem was, because of Katy's relatively sheltered upbringing, she didn't have a huge knowledge of mainstream music so had no idea who to approach to help her in the next important stage of her musical career. It was time for Katy to turn on the radio and discover a world outside Christian rock and pop . . .

3

Katy Perry is Born

S he was just sixteen years old, but already young Katy
Hudson had seen the darker side of the music industry,
as her first dream of music stardom had fallen at the first
hurdle when Red Hill Records went bankrupt. It must have
been hard to start over, knowing that the album that she
had worked so hard on was now little more than a pile of
discarded CDs lying in a dumpster somewhere in Nashville.
But Katy knew she wanted to be a singer and songwriter
more than anything in the world, and she was determined
this first failure was not going to hold her back. But what
would be her next move? Christian rock hadn't worked out,
so maybe more mainstream music was a better choice for
the enthusiastic teen.

Aside from Madonna and a few other artists, Katy didn't
have a huge frame of reference when it came to pop music.
She started to listen to more and more music, and soon had
some favourites, beginning with the Beach Boys' legendary
1966 album *Pet Sounds*. The eleventh studio album from the
Californian band, it is widely regarded as not only their best,
but also one of the most influential music albums of all time.

NME, *The Times* and rock bible *Mojo* magazine all ranked it the number one album of all time, while *Rolling Stone* placed it at number two in their list of The 500 Greatest Albums of All Time in 2003 (it was beaten to the number one spot by The Beatles' *Sergeant Pepper's Lonely Hearts Club Band*).

It was a great choice for Santa Barbara girl Katy, as the Beach Boys had developed a unique Californian sound that must have reminded her of sunny days on the beach near her home. Packed with elaborate vocal harmonies and musical instruments you wouldn't necessarily expect on a pop album (harpsichord, flute and even whistles), it features some of the band's best songs including 'Wouldn't It Be Nice', the tear-jerking 'God Only Knows' (regarded as one of the best songs ever written) and 'I Just Wasn't Made for These Times'.

Knowing her parents wouldn't approve of some of the music she was listening to, Katy snuck CDs into her bedroom and played them quietly, even going so far as to push her duvet against the gap under her bedroom door to muffle the sound of the devil's music. One track her mum and dad would have been horrified to learn that she was listening to was one that was to change her perspective on music entirely.

'It was a moment where everything kind of went in slow motion,' Katy told *Observer* reporter Sheryl Garratt of the moment she first heard the special song. 'The clouds moved away, the sun started shining and I was like: "I've found it! I've found an artist I want to be like!" Everybody has that one person they want to be, that poster on the wall: Elvis, Madonna . . . '

And who had captured Katy's imagination so strongly?

'For me it was a song called "Killer Queen". I wanted to be like Freddie Mercury.'

A flamboyant British rocker was an odd choice of role model for a Californian teenage girl, perhaps, but also a perfect one. Katy first heard 'Killer Queen' at a friend's sleepover, and she was instantly hooked. 'He is pretty much my biggest influence/idol,' she told the *Star Scoop* in an interview. 'He's very theatrical and boisterous and he always said what he thought and really didn't give a f*** what anybody thought about when he walked on the stage with a crown and looked like a queen.'

Freddie, of course, had lived a life that was worlds away from the one Katy knew. Born in Zanzibar (his birth name was Farrokh Bulsara) in 1946, and raised in India, Freddie moved with his family to Middlesex in England when he was seventeen and he studied art at Isleworth Polytechnic and Ealing Art College before getting a job at Heathrow airport. It was definitely a far cry from Katy's sunny Santa Barbara Christian upbringing – Freddie and his family practised Zoroastrianism, based on the teachings of a Persian prophet, which Katy's parents would likely have disapproved of.

After joining a couple of rock bands that went nowhere, Freddie met Roger Taylor and Brian May in 1970 and formed the band Queen, and he changed his last name from Bulsara to Mercury. As well as both changing their names in their careers, Freddie and Katy have other things in common. Freddie was a skilled songwriter, writing or co-writing some of Queen's most famous songs, including 'Bohemian Rhapsody', 'Somebody to Love', 'We Are the Champions' and Katy's favourite, 'Killer Queen'. Like Katy, he could weave

complex lyrics into a short pop song (never better demon-
strated than in 'Bohemian Rhapsody': 'Mama, just killed a
man / put a gun against his head / pulled the trigger, now
he's dead . . . '), and he also had a flair for the dramatic that
made him mesmerising to watch.

There's no doubt that Katy picked up on Freddie
Mercury's renowned showmanship. He was known for his
extrovert, flamboyant and deliciously bonkers concert persona, as he preened up and down the stage, performing
songs in a captivatingly theatrical manner, whether parad-
ing in leather trousers and studded cap or royally storm-
ing about in ermine-style cape and crown. 'Of all the more
theatrical rock performers, Freddie took it further than the
rest,' his pal David Bowie once commented. 'He took it over
the edge. And, of course, I always admired a man who wears
tights. He was definitely a man who could hold the audience in the palm of his hand.' Whether it was getting more
than 72,000 people to clap along to 'Radio Ga Ga' at Live Aid,
or wearing a dress and hoovering while singing 'I Want to
Break Free' in a pop video, Freddie Mercury knew how to
make you never forget him, his stunning voice or his memorable performances.

Sadly, Freddie died, aged forty-five, in 1991. So by the
time Katy discovered his music, he had already left us, but
her own vibrant stage costumes, outrageous concert performances and clever, fun music videos are a tribute to the
artist who so bewitched a teenage California girl.

Of course, while Katy could see from Freddie how to wow
an audience and express herself in her costumes, she still
needed to develop her own sound and style of music so she

could then show record executives what she could do. When she wasn't listening to Queen, Katy listened to artists whom she saw had strong, female perspectives on music, including Gwen Stefani of No Doubt, Shirley Manson of Garbage, as well as the Cranberries, Joan Jett, Cyndi Lauper and Alanis Morissette, whose album *Jagged Little Pill* would lead Katy down another unexpected path.

Like Katy, Alanis Morissette had tried to break into music stardom with a visit to Nashville. Following the release of her first two albums in her native Canada, she felt nothing much was happening to her music career so she went to Music City USA but had no better luck there than Katy had done. From there, Alanis tried Los Angeles, where she met a series of producers, and befriended one in particular, Glen Ballard, who went on to work with her on *Jagged Little Pill*, the album that made Alanis an international star in 1995 when Katy was just eleven years old.

When Katy first heard the album, she was intrigued. 'She [Alanis] was totally a fly on every girl's wall,' Katy told journalist Sophie Harris, 'and that's what I wanted to do, sing about honest things.'

One night, Katy saw Alanis's producer being interviewed on VH1: 'I thought, you know what, I want to work with him,' she told *Star Scoop*. 'So the next day, I came into the studio (where I was working) and I said, "I want to work with this guy named Glen Ballard."' The producer Katy was working with at the time made lots of phone calls and pulled every string he could to get Katy a meeting with Ballard in Los Angeles. 'I had my dad drive me up to LA. I said, "Dad, stay in the car. I'm just gonna go in, play a song for this guy and come back out." And I did, and I guess it went well, because I got the call the next day.'

Glen Ballard was a great person for her to meet. He began his music career in 1975 working in Los Angeles, writing songs for Kiki Dee. He then worked for MCA, writing a variety of songs in the Eighties (originally for $100 a week) for artists including George Benson, the Pointer Sisters and Patti Austin. By the time Katy was born in 1984, Ballard was becoming a force to be reckoned with in the music industry. He co-wrote Michael Jackson's 'Man in the Mirror', wrote Curtis Stigers' big hit 'I Wonder Why' and Aerosmith's 'Pink', co-wrote Christina Aguilera's 'The Voice Within' and won three Grammys for his work with Alanis Morissette on *Jagged Little Pill*.

His work with Alanis had made him a much-sought-after writer and producer, and Glen and Katy soon settled into working together on an album they were sure would be a hit. Aged just seventeen, Katy packed her bags and moved to Los Angeles, leaving her family behind in Santa Barbara, so she could work on writing and recording songs. For months, she and Glen worked, and with his help she was offered a record deal with Island Def Jam, the record company that boasts Bon Jovi, Mariah Carey, Florence and the Machine, Jennifer Lopez and Rihanna among its artists.

Starting in 2002, Katy and Glen worked hard for two years on a rock album for her, with a planned release date of 2005. Once again, however, she was going to be disappointed. On hearing it, Island Def Jam decided not to release the album, and Katy was back on her own, with no producer, no recording contract, and no clue what to do next. Not all of her music was entirely lost, however – some of Katy's collaborations were posted on her MySpace page, including 'Box', 'Long Shot' and 'Diamonds', while another track she recorded, 'Simple', popped up on the soundtrack to the teen movie *The Sisterhood of the Traveling Pants*.

Luckily, Katy didn't take no for an answer, and she kept on going, meeting record executives in the hope that one would sign her up. Now nineteen, she decided to give herself until the age of twenty-five to make it big – if it hadn't happened then, it never would, she reasoned. She also made a decision to change her name in the hope that a new name would bring new success. Katy Hudson was out – partly to avoid confusion with actress Kate Hudson, who by 2004 was the established star of *Almost Famous* and *How to Lose a Guy in 10 Days* – and Katy Perry was born (Perry being Katy's mother's maiden name).

With her new name and bouncy persona, Katy was unstoppable despite knocks along the way. 'The first time I got signed, they brought me in a room with three other girls they signed at the same time,' she recalled to journalist Rob Sheffield about her years in the musical wilderness. 'They sat us down and said, "Maybe one of you will ever make a record. One of you will actually take a swing [at it]. The other two can go back to Middle America and pop out babies."' Not exactly encouraging words, but Katy wasn't to be deterred from her dream.

In 2004, just before her twentieth birthday, she signed to her third record company, Columbia Records, the famous recording home of David Bowie, Johnny Cash, Destiny's Child, Prince and Paul McCartney. Rather than promote her as a

solo singer, however, Columbia decided to pair her with the production team The Matrix, thinking she would be a perfect female vocalist for their album. The Matrix are Lauren Christy, her husband Graham Edwards and Scott Spock. Together they have co-written and produced songs for Avril Lavinge (including the hit 'Complicated'), Britney Spears ('Shadow'), Shakira ('Don't Bother') and boy-band Busted ('A Present for Everyone'). Their plan was to make an album with a handful of unknown singers – Katy and London-born A.K.A. among them – that would be an instant hit.

It looked like things were on the up for Katy at last. In September 2004, while working with The Matrix, she was picked as The Next Big Thing by US music magazine *Blender*. In journalist Nick Duerden's profile on her, she talked about her collaboration with The Matrix. 'At first, I thought "Crap! There goes my credibility!"' she said of working with the group. 'They've worked with some brilliant people, but also people who are hardly artists at all. But if people buy the record, that's all the credibility I need.'

The Matrix member Scott Spock explained to *Billboard* magazine what they were working on. 'This is a creative experiment in the way modern pop music is made. We've cast this album like a movie. We've chosen to work with Katy and A.K.A. because of their backgrounds, their abilities and what they have to say. Both come across with a talent that reflects a very unique area of music.'

It seemed like an interesting project, and one that allowed time for Katy to work on her own solo album for Columbia. 'We wanted artists who had their own careers, but were willing to be involved with this,' said Lauren Christy. 'They can go off as solo performers, then come back, write together and create with us.' Christy remembered how Katy had first come to their attention, with Glen Ballard suggesting they check out the girl he had worked with for two years. 'We saw a video Katy made with her band using a handheld camera and she was just riveting. You couldn't take your eyes off her.'

The trio worked with Katy on the album, but once again her hopes were dashed when Columbia Records decided to shelve the project and not release it. (Following Katy's solo success at the end of the decade, in 2009 The Matrix released the album on their own label, Let's Hear It Records.) Undaunted, she continued to work on her solo album for the label, but that was then put on hold, too. Katy's current manager, Bradford Cobb, continued the story to *Billboard* magazine: 'Columbia was never really willing to embrace Katy's vision. They were not willing to let her drive. Here was this ambitious young woman with a clear picture of who she was and the willingness to work hard, and Columbia just wouldn't put her in the driving seat.' Although eighty per cent of her solo album was finished, it was never completed: 'We got the masters back and then started looking for a new home,' Cobb remembers.

'It was super-discouraging,' Katy remembered to the *Scotsman* a few years later. 'I got so close on records that I would bring a copy of it and the artwork and I would show my friends and say "Can you believe it? It's finally happening!" And two weeks later I would get the call that it wasn't happening.'

The rejection by Columbia was soul-destroying. 'Nobody at those labels [Island, Columbia] got what she was about,' says Glen Ballard. 'She had talent, personality, humour, a sense of fashion. They didn't know what to do with it.'

It looked like Katy was on her own again. She didn't sit at home and sulk, however ('If I fail, I dust myself down and start again'). Nobody may have wanted her recording in a studio, but she knew she had to keep herself busy while she waited for the next offer of a recording contract to come along. By the time 2006 began, Katy was alone in sprawling Los Angeles, without an album. Down but not out, she took a series of jobs to pay the rent and soon found herself working at Taxi Music.

'After I'd lost my second record deal, I had to take odd jobs,' she told journalist Adrian Thrills. 'I had one for a music publisher, where I had to sit in a cubicle and listen to other people's songs all day. Most were horrible, and I just wanted to warn the singers about what they were getting into.'

Her boss, Michael Laskow, still remembers her. 'A typical day for Katy would be probably listening to several dozen songs to find out which songs and artists were good enough to pass on to a record company or publisher,' he says.

It must have been awful to sit there in a small cubicle with only her iMac computer for company, as other girls with attitude like Avril Lavigne got record deals and had hit songs in the chart while Katy was sitting answering phones. 'I saw other girls come and go. I wondered if there would still be space for me. But I knew I was different. I'm a big goofball who speaks her mind, and there's always room in music for someone with a strong vision.'

Katy kept herself busy, supplying guest vocals on a song called 'Goodbye for Now' by the Christian rock-metal band P.O.D. (it stands for 'Payable on Death') and she also appeared in the video for Carbon Leaf's song 'Learn to Fly', as a girl trying to get to one of their gigs. Neither boosted her profile very much, but Katy wasn't to know that two events around the corner were going to change her life – both musically and personally.

On Wednesday, 8 February 2006, Katy Perry got up for her job at Taxi Music, just like every other Wednesday. However, while she was sitting in their Calabasas office taking phone calls and helping out, a few miles south-east of her at the Staples Center, preparations were being made for one of music's biggest events of the year, the Grammy Awards.

Inside the circular building that is home to the Los Angeles Lakers basketball team in Downtown LA, glasses were being washed ready to be filled with champagne, red carpet was being laid out for the numerous stars to walk along, and fans queued outside to see who would arrive for the forty-eighth Grammy Awards. Madonna, Stevie Wonder, Alicia Keys, Coldplay, U2, Mary J. Blige and Paul McCartney were among the performers that night while U2, *American Idol* winner Kelly Clarkson and Mariah Carey were among those who took home awards.

In the crowd of musicians and singers was Virgin Music's Chris Anokute. A senior A&R executive for the label (part of the Capital Music Group), Chris's job is to be responsible for talent-scouting for new musicians and then overseeing the artistic development of an artist. Chris was at the Grammys with his boss, Jason Flom, who introduced him to Angelica Cob-Baehler, a publicity executive at Katy's old label, Columbia Records.

In an interview with Jan Blumentrath, Chris remembered hearing Katy's name for the first time. 'She [Angelica] was telling me about this girl Katy Perry that was signed to Columbia. She said "She's a singer-songwriter. She's incredible. She used to be a Christian singer and Columbia doesn't really know what to do with her and they are about to drop her." I said, "Well, send me the music!"'

Angelica sent Chris a DVD of Katy and three demos of songs she had recorded for Columbia, for the album that was never released. 'I put in the DVD,' says Chris. 'It was an independent low-budget video for a song called "Simple", an early song she did with Glen Ballard. For some reason I thought, "Oh my god, she is a superstar". She reminded me of Alanis Morissette. I listened to two other songs on the demo. One was "Waking Up in Vegas" and when I heard that I thought, "This is a number one record!"'

Chris took the demo to his boss's office and told Jason Flom that he had found the next Avril Lavinge or Alanis. 'When I played him the demos he wasn't sure if it was good enough,' Chris told Jan Blumentrath. 'To be honest, he didn't really get it. More importantly, he had heard about her through the years and this wasn't the first time Katy Perry had been dropped – she'd been dropped before from Island/Def Jam. But because I was so passionate about it, Jason decided to come to a showcase in LA at the Viper Room.'

A nightclub on the Sunset Strip that was once part-owned by Johnny Depp, the Viper Room has always been known as a hang-out for Hollywood's young actors, and a place to catch rock acts, both established and new. Notorious as the place where young actor River Phoenix died after a drug overdose in 1993, collapsing on the pavement outside, it's a black-fronted building with dark doors and a black canopy over an entrance that leads to a small stage, busy bar and cramped area for the audience. In this always hot and sweaty venue (for both the crowd and the performers), Katy had managed to secure enough time to perform a short set of her unrecorded songs.

According to Chris Anokute, however, Flom was unimpressed. 'The showcase wasn't that good, to be honest,' Chris told Blumentrath. 'Although I saw the star talent in her.' He was not going to let one mediocre performance put him off selling Katy to his boss. 'I'm so passionate about it that every single week I'm beating him [Flom] up, trying to convince him to sign her, saying "Jason, we'll find the record, we'll develop her, we'll figure it out! There is something special about her, I know she is a star. Who cares that she was dropped?"'

Chris and Angelica Cob-Baehler – who was moving over to Virgin Records and wanted to bring Katy with her – continued to pester Flom. Eventually they must have worn him down, as seven weeks later, Flom emailed Chris. 'Jason emails me, "It's great, what are we waiting for? Let's sign the girl." So we offered her a deal.'

Katy had no idea what had been going on up to this point. But one day, sitting in the Taxi Music office, she got the call that would change everything. 'Jason Flom called me. That day I went out for coffee and never went back.'

Finally, Katy had a record deal with a mentor who could truly see her potential as an artist and a chart star. By the end of 2006, life was looking up, and Katy was not only looking at a new record deal but also a new relationship.

She had been asked to appear in the video for a song called 'Cupid's Chokehold' by a hip hop band named Gym Class Heroes. Formed in 1997, the group is made up of MC Travis 'Travie' McCoy, drummer Matt McGinley, guitarist Disashi Lumumba-Kasongo and bassist Eric Roberts. It was Travis whom Katy became friendly with as they filmed the video, which tells the story of Travis's failed loves, who have all been picked out by a cheeky little cupid, and the one love (played by Katy) whom he chooses without being hit by Cupid's arrow first.

It wasn't long before Katy and Travis were a little more than friends, like the couple they play in the video. Travis's star was on the rise – 'Cupid's Chokehold' reached number four in the *Billboard* charts in March 2007 and Katy was working hard to prove herself at Virgin/Capitol Music, but they would hang out whenever they could find the time.

'We weren't really together [to begin with],' Katy told journalist Rob Sheffield in 2008. 'It was casual. But soulless hooking up didn't seem so hot to me. I always wanted to have a romance. I said "Excuse me, I've been coming to a number of your shows in the greater Los Angeles area for quite some time now. I've been your Penny Lane [the groupie from the movie *Almost Famous*] long enough, and now I want to be your Grace Kelly."'

'She's opulent,' Travis said in the same interview. 'I was smitten as soon as she walked in the room – she's a girl who demands attention. I have no game whatsoever, so I decided, "I'm just gonna ignore the s*** out of her". In essence, that worked!'

Soon, the pair were inseparable, and while waiting for

her record deal to begin at Captiol, Katy found her name appearing alongside that of Travis's in the tabloids. On the outside things were looking up, but not everything about the new relationship was easy, as Travis himself revealed to the *Daily Mirror* in 2008. 'There was this really, really dark point about two years ago where I just hit rock bottom . . . and I called Katy who was in LA at the time and said to her, "Do you mind coming out and keeping me company, I'm not in a good state of mind right now." And I honestly think if she had not come – I really don't think I would be here right now. Without even talking, she just listened. I truly believed that saved my life.'

The year of 2007 was looking very promising, and it seemed as though Katy's dreams of both stardom and romance were coming true. Her story so far sounded like the plot of a Hollywood movie, even to Katy. 'Capitol Records picked me up and decided they wanted to make a *Pretty Woman* story out of me . . . without the prostitution,' she joked. A true pop star was being born.

4

I Kissed a Girl

As 2007 began, Katy Perry had a boyfriend, Travis McCoy, and, even better than that, a recording contract with Capitol Records. Plans were in place for Katy to start writing and recording songs for her first album and Chris Anokute, who oversaw Katy's progress, decided to team her up with songwriter, producer and remixer Dr Luke. She had actually worked with him before, back when she had a record deal at Columbia, but they had never finished what they started. It was a good match, as Dr Luke – real name Lukasz Gottwald – who began his music career performing weekly on the TV show *Saturday Night Live* as the in-house band's lead guitarist, has since worked on massive chart hits including Kelly Clarkson's 'Since U Been Gone', Pink's 'Who Knew', Avril Lavigne's 'Girlfriend' and songs for Britney Spears' album *Circus*. He was experienced at writing and producing with young female singers, and when Capitol's Jason Flom convinced him to go back into the studio with Katy, they were soon recording the first tracks of what was to be Katy's breakthrough album.

They wrote and recorded 'I Kissed a Girl' and 'Hot n

Cold', while Katy also sat down and wrote two songs with writer/producer Greg Wells, 'Ur So Gay' and 'Mannequin'. She certainly had a lot of material to choose from – since her first failed record deal when she was fifteen, she had written more than sixty songs and kept all of them. Over the first few months of 2007, Katy went through them all and, with the help of her team at Capitol, soon the line-up of songs for her first album there was beginning to form.

Rather than just release the album onto an unsuspecting public, Capitol decided to mount a special campaign for Katy, beginning by introducing her memorable personality and image to everyone. 'The campaign really started in November 2007 with the release of the video for "Ur So Gay",' Capitol Records executive Bob Semanovich told reporter Cortney Harding. 'We were going for something that was playful and fun, a way to introduce her and get people talking.' They released the single as a digital EP, so it would gather online buzz as well as being heard on the radio.

It was the video, directed by Walter May, which was most memorable. 'Ur So Gay' has Katy, in a Fifties-style polka-dot dress, sitting on some fake grass with plastic daisies around her (sort of like the *Teletubbies* set), with animated clouds floating by. As she sings and plays her guitar, the video's story is played out by Ken- and Barbie-style dolls. The doll-man, a musician with a love for hybrid cars and soya coffee, meets the doll-woman in a coffee shop but then goes off with his male pal; the next thing we see is the woman dyeing and cutting her hair, going from blonde to black (and looking a bit like Katy herself) to seduce him. The musician meets her again and comes back to her place, where they drink a few bottles of wine, then he passes out and she removes his trousers . . . only to discover he really is a doll in that department, with no genitals at all! It's a really cute mini-movie, backed by a fun song that has Katy's trademark sparky lyrics.

'I came up with the concept of the dolls in the video and wanted to make sure it was seen as a tongue-in-cheek diss track,' Katy told *Billboard* magazine. 'It [the video] started getting passed around and really took off when *Blender* [magazine] reported on it.'

'We put out "Ur So Gay" as a single as a kind of introduction because we thought we'd have to build her story all over again,' Capitol's Chris Anokute told HitQuarters.com. 'It was kind of a novelty song. We never had plans to go to radio, we just wanted to put it out online and see what the attraction was. We shot the low-budget video and the response was great.'

With lines such as 'I hope you hang yourself with your H&M scarf / while jacking off listening to Mozart' and 'You're so gay and you don't even like boys' (neither of which, to most listeners, seemed especially shocking), the single was slapped with a 'Parental Advisory' sticker when it was released in the USA. This has almost become something of a badge of honour in the music industry – the sticker is placed on music considered to feature profane language and/or sexual references. It was first introduced in 1985, following pressure from a group called the Parents Music Resource Center, founded by four wives of Washington politicians, including Tipper Gore, wife of Al Gore. They released a list called the 'Filthy Fifteen' – fifteen songs they found particularly offensive at the time that included Prince's enjoyably rude 'Darling Nikki', Madonna's 'Dress You Up', Cyndi Lauper's ode to masturbation, 'She Bop' and 'Sugar Walls', sung by the previously innocent Scottish pop poppet Sheena Easton (another song written by naughty old Prince).

Since then, the sticker has appeared on everything from Guns N' Roses' classic album *Appetite for Destruction*, Madonna's *Erotica*, Jennifer Lopez's album *J.Lo* and *You've Come a Long Way, Baby* by Fatboy Slim. Katy was in good company, and even though some stores in the USA (including supermarket giant Walmart) refuse to sell records with the sticker on it, research has shown that having the 'parental advisory' notice on a song or album will often encourage people to buy it.

Like many people, Katy didn't regard her song as shocking, and, in fact, described it as her 'soft hello' to the world of pop. It wasn't supposed to set the tone of the album or show all she could do as an artist; instead, it was aimed at the people who had already discovered her on the internet, via her MySpace page, and was an introduction to just part of her charm for everyone else. It certainly got her noticed. A year after she started work with Capitol Records, the buzz on Katy was finally building, with Michael Slezak of influential magazine *Entertainment Weekly* writing a glowing tribute to her in January 2008: 'I know the lyrics to Katy Perry's "Ur So Gay" are eighteen different kinds of wrong – the opening line about what she'd like her wayward beau to do with his H&M scarf is not for the faint of heart, nor is it entirely safe for work – but I can't stop playing this jaunty little ditty on repeat (despite its misspelled title). I don't care that there's almost no chance corporate radio will embrace a song that includes the lines: "I can't believe I fell in love / With someone who wears full make-up and / You're so gay and you don't even like boys." I am out and proud fan of "Ur So Gay". Listen for yourself and tell me if you don't love it, too.'

Katy also had a very special person heaping praise on her debut – Madonna. When she was interviewed on Arizona's Johnjay & Rich morning radio show, the pop queen said 'Ur So Gay' was her 'favourite song right now', and she also mentioned it on Ryan Seacrest's national radio show.

However, it wasn't all so positive. Marguerite French of the UGO website described the song as being packed with 'catchphrase-homophobia', while allmusic.com said it was 'gay-baiting' and described Katy as having a 'vile wild child persona'. The song made Virgin Media's list of the Top 10 Most Offensive Songs, alongside more 'shocking' tunes such as the Sex Pistols' 'God Save the Queen', Prodigy's 'Smack My Bitch Up' and Bodycount's 'Cop Killer'. It was also criticised by British activist Peter Tatchell, who said the song 'can be read as implicitly demeaning gay people'.

'I am sure Katy would get a critical reception if she expressed comparable sentiments in a song called "Ur So Black, Jewish or Disabled",' he commented. With other criticisms of the lyrics cropping up regularly, Katy was forced to defend her song. 'We live in a very metrosexual world,' she explained in her defence to *The Times*. 'You know, a girl might walk into a bar, meet a boy, and discover he's more manicured than she is. And they can't figure it out. Is he wearing foundation and a bit of bronzer? But he's buying me drinks at the same time! I'm not saying you're so gay, you're so lame. I'm saying, you're so gay, but I don't understand it because you don't like boys!'

Whether newspapers loved or hated the song, it certainly got Katy noticed. She was offered a cameo role as herself in the US TV series *Wildfire*, a family drama set against a backdrop of horse-racing, in an episode called *Life's Too Short* that aired on 10 March 2008, and followed that by going on a two-month tour of radio stations, to promote her upcoming album and her second single, a song called 'I Kissed a Girl', written by Katy along with Dr Luke, Max Martin and Cathy Dennis.

According to Katy, there was a definite inspiration for the song, which, as its title suggests, talks about her kissing a girl. She was flipping through a magazine when she came across a photo of Scarlett Johansson, the star of *Lost in Translation* and *Iron Man 2*, and she told boyfriend Travis McCoy that, if Scarlett walked into the room right then and there and wanted to make out with Katy, she would do it. From there, the idea for the song developed and became Katy's first real hit record.

It was released on 6 May 2008. Following on from 'Ur So Gay', it was a controversial choice for Capitol Records to make, as the song once again featured lyrics that would raise a few eyebrows. As well as the chorus, in which Katy proclaims 'I kissed a girl and I liked it / the taste of her cherry chap-stick', the song goes on to say 'No, I don't even know your name / it doesn't matter / you're my experimental game / just human nature.' Uh oh.

'We were aware of the politics, and there was some concern about releasing "Ur So Gay" and then "I Kissed a

Girl"', says Katy's manager, Brandon Cobb. 'We had two groups that never agreed on anything who were both mad at us,' he continues, referring to America's religious right-wing groups and gay rights groups, who both criticised the song and Katy herself.

The reactions to the song were often extreme. At the Havens Corners Church in Ohio, a sign was placed outside that read 'I kissed a girl and I liked it, then I went to Hell'. The senior pastor of the church, David Allinson, told *NBC News* he wanted to remind teenagers that the Bible denounces homosexuality: 'If anyone's seen the video and understands how lewd and suggestive the video is for this song, that is not something young people should go toward.' (In response, someone sprayed three words of graffiti over the sign: 'God Adores You'.)

A website run by Focus on the Family (a US Christian group) reviewed the single and decided Katy was 'living down to a damaging, demeaning, "girls gone wild" stereotype'. However, the writer goes on to say he hopes that perhaps the 'good' Katy will 'come to her senses and recall the wisdom of her [Christian] youth'. Meanwhile *Slant* magazine criticised the lyrics, saying: '[The song] isn't problematic because it promotes homosexuality, but because its appropriation of the gay lifestyle exists for the sole purpose of garnering attention – both from Perry's boyfriend and her audience.'

The song was even banned from some stores, and there were rumours it was banned from Singapore radio altogether. In Texas, three cheerleaders were suspended from performing at football games after they twirled their batons to 'I Kissed a Girl' in front of a crowd before a match, while in Brazil, teacher Marcio Barros was fired from his job after he used the song in a lesson for twelve-to-fourteen-year-old students and the headmaster decided it promoted homosexuality and alcohol.

Even the title got some people up in arms. Singer-songwriter Jill Sobule had written a song called 'I Kissed a Girl' back in 1995, and she was furious that another song was out there – and a controversial one, at that – with the same name. In an interview with The Rumpus, a culture website, Jill let rip with her thoughts:

'When Katy Perry's version came out I started getting tons of inquiries about what I thought. Some folks (and protective friends) were angry, and wondered why she took my title and made it into this kind of "girls gone wild" thing. Others, including my mother, were excited because they thought I would somehow make some money out of it. Unfortunately you can't copyright a title . . . bummer.

'As a musician I have always refrained from criticising another artist. I was, "Well, good for her." It did bug me a little bit, however, when she said she came up with the idea for the title in a dream. In truth, she wrote it with a team of professional writers and was signed by the very same guy that signed me in 1995. I have not mentioned that in interviews as I don't want to sound bitter or petty . . . cause, that's not me. Okay, maybe, if I really think about it, there were a few jealous and pissed off moments. So here goes, for the first time in an interview: "F*** you, Katy Perry, you f***ing stupid, maybe 'not good for the gays,' title thieving, haven't heard much else, so not quite sure if you're talented, f***ing little slut."'

Strong words, but, believe it or not, they were misinterpreted by the media that picked up on Jill's rant. She had actually prefaced her speech with a wink, and was having fun with her fans and readers of the site, littering her words with profanities she doesn't usually use, and, as she later explained, she 'rambled on . . . completely in jest'. Unfortunately other news media that had picked up the story had failed to include her wink, so took the whole thing seriously, adding Jill to the list of people they reported didn't like Katy's song.

'The song is just about drunken curiosity, not a call to change a girl's sexual orientation,' says Katy, defending the lyrics. 'I'm talking about the way girls are really touchy-feely and sisterly. Especially when we're growing up. We're holding hands, we're having sleepovers, we're doing choreographed dance moves in our pyjamas, we're painting each other's nails and practising kissing on our arms – or maybe practising kissing on one another,' she told the *Observer*'s Sheryl Garratt. 'It wasn't something we were doing for the sake of anybody else because we were scared of boys. I know I was scared of boys! My first kiss with a boy – he almost swallowed me alive! I wish I had kissed that girl I had the girl-crush on when I was growing up. I would have been much more prepared for my dating life.'

Her parents weren't best pleased with the song's lyrics, either. The *Daily Mail* reported that Katy's mum Mary went mad when she heard the song, and she gave a few angry quotes to the media that were picked up in the press around the world: 'I hate the song,' she said. 'It clearly promotes homosexuality and its message is shameful and disgusting. Katy knows how I feel. We are a very outspoken family. I can't even listen to that song. The first time I heard it I was in total shock. When it comes on the radio I bow my head and pray. Katy is our daughter and we love her but we strongly disagree with how she is conducting herself at the moment. We cannot cut her out of our lives as she is our child – but she knows we disagree strongly with what she is doing and the message she is promoting regarding homosexuality which the Bible clearly states is a sin. But the Bible also promotes understanding and forgiveness, which I keep reminding myself.'

It wasn't only the song that had upset her parents – they had also noticed Katy's provocative stage and video attire. 'Some [of her clothes] are too revealing and her father has had words with her about it. Like any child she is going through a period of rebellion.' (Sensibly, Katy dismissed the reports of her parents' comments as nonsense, inferring that her mother had been caught out by a tabloid reporter and wasn't aware that what she said would be relayed around the world: 'My parents are definitely supportive and happy for my success.')

If it was a rebellion on Katy's behalf, it was a rebellion that was working, despite the bad press and her parents' misgivings. There was no avoiding the song's success. By 13 June, 'I Kissed a Girl' was the number one best-selling pop song on iTunes, the number one most requested song on numerous radio stations across the USA, including New York's influential Z100, and the video had over two million hits in its first two weeks on MySpace, after it premiered on 21 May.

A bigger budget had been spent on Katy's video this

time around, and it was shot by Kinga Burza, who had also worked with Kate Nash and The Thrills. It features Katy lying on red satin sheets in a gold dress while she sings, and also has scenes of her having pillow fights (feathers going everywhere) in a room full of women, and splashing about in a corset with some gal pals (there is no kissing though) . . . but at the end we see Katy in bed with a man (a cameo performance from real-life boyfriend Travis McCoy) and realise everything that went before was a dream.

Real life was much more fun than any dream for Katy, however. She watched 'I Kissed a Girl' charge up the charts, becoming the 1000th number one song of the rock era, and also having the distinction of being the first song since Gnarls Barkley's 'Crazy' to be included on the mainstream Top 40, Rhythmic, Adult Top 40 and Alternative charts at the same time. It spent five weeks at the top in Britain, and topped the charts in more than thirty countries, becoming the tenth-best-selling single of the twenty-first century. Meanwhile the raunchy video had over 25 million views on YouTube and – the ultimate compliment, perhaps – scores of parodies of the song started popping up on the website, too. Katy had hit the big time, and things were only going to get bigger . . . and more controversial.

5

One of the Boys

By June 2008, Katy's single 'I Kissed a Girl' was sitting at the top of the US charts and her face was often appearing in magazines, with the Santa Barbara twenty-three-year-old often being tipped as 'the one to watch'. People lined up to comment on this new, fun pop star – including the *Lost in Translation* movie star Scarlett Johansson, who when told that Katy said she inspired the song 'I Kissed a Girl', told *People* magazine that she was flattered. 'It's flattering, but my lips are kind of taken,' she said, referring to her relationship with actor Ryan Reynolds, whom she married later that year. Meanwhile, when Katy appeared on US TV talk-show *The View*, and sang her hit song, one of the show's presenters, comedienne and Oscar-winning actress Whoopi Goldberg, gave her a big kiss.

While the *LA Times* said Katy had a 'potty mouth' and that she was 'carelessly appropriating gay culture in her songs', other critics took 'I Kissed a Girl' for the fun, pop single that it was. As it topped charts all over the world, Katy's management realised it was time to show everyone what a great live performer she was, and get her album ready for release, too.

The album was entitled *One of the Boys*, and included her two singles, 'Ur So Gay' and 'I Kissed a Girl'. Featuring Katy on the cover in a Fifties-style red corset top and high-waisted shorts, sunning herself on a lounger in a plastic-looking garden (complete with fake flowers and a white picket fence behind her), the album was released on 17 June 2008 in the USA. It must have been amazing for Katy, after almost nine years of trying, to finally see her own album on the shelves of record stores – and, indeed, flying off those shelves. But she had little opportunity to enjoy the moment of her first big success, as it was time for her to pack her bags – and her guitar – and hit the road on tour.

Instead of booking Katy to perform solo in small venues around the USA, Capitol Records had another idea. They still needed to build up Katy's fan-base and get as many teenagers as possible to know about her, so they signed her up to join the Warped Tour, which began on 20 June in Pomona, California, and then toured the USA and Canada, playing different cities – such as San Francisco, Denver, Dallas, Miami, Montreal and Milwaukee – every night until the tour finished on 17 August, back in California. It was a lot of performances for a new singer like Katy, and quite a production, too – over 100 different acts were on the tour, so there was no space for egos or timewasters.

The Warped Tour began in 1994 as a music and extreme sports festival. Held in car parks and fields big enough to contain the stages, it was originally a showcase for punk performers, but by the year 2000 had grown into a large festival boasting up to ten stages and as many as 100 bands per day. Each band got to play for up to thirty-five minutes on one of the stages (with the order of performances posted on a huge inflatable notice board), and the concert would run from around 11 a.m. to 9 p.m. There are some interesting behind-the-scenes rules – on each tour there is a band that is designated the 'BBQ Band', and has to cook the food on the tour in return for being allowed to perform. There is also a band that works as the set-up crew for the tour during the day, and, as a reward for this labour, gets to perform on stage each night.

The Warped Tour isn't just about music, either. There is always a half pipe (curved ramp) for skateboarders and bikers set up at every venue, plus booths selling band merchandise and products that will appeal to festival-goers. The tour has even become eco-friendly, with a stage that runs on solar power, tour-buses filled with bio-diesel fuel and recyclable take-away cartons at the food stands.

By the time Katy joined it in 2008, the Warped Tour, sponsored by Vans shoes, was well established and no longer just for punk bands. Metalcore, pop-punk, pop, reggae, hip hop and ska bands were also on the line-up (leading to some controversy in the punk press as the tour was criticised for becoming too commercial). The acts performed on different stages – the main stage boasted bands including pop-punk act Paramore (perhaps best known for their song 'Decode', which was featured in the movie *Twilight*), California rock group The Vandals, and Gym Class Heroes (led by Katy's boyfriend Travis, of course). There was also the Ernie Ball stage, the Smartpunk.com stage, a Battle of the Bands stage and the Hurley.com stage, which was to be Katy's home for the eight weeks of the tour.

It was quite a male-dominated atmosphere for a young female singer but Katy didn't seem fazed by the sweaty road-ies, snarling punk stars and unglamorous locations (after all, singing in a car park isn't exactly Wembley Stadium). Each and every day, she got up, did radio and print interviews to promote the album, went along to that day's location and signed hundreds of autographs before stepping up to per-form on stage. To finish off each performance, she threw herself into the crowd in front of her. And they loved it. Her inspiration for rocking out with the boys was probably Gwen Stefani, who, with her band No Doubt, had joined the Warped Tour herself back in 2000.

'Warped is gruelling and hot, but I'm ready to survive it – even without the showers,' Katy told reporters covering the shows, not forgetting to mention the tour's frugal backstage facilities. 'Gwen Stefani did the tour and she looked fabulous hopping around on stage in her little polka-dot dresses. You can find YouTube clips of her up there and all the girls in the audience are going nuts. I'm so channelling that!'

It *was* gruelling work, especially because no act knows their time slot until the day and the schedule is punishing. It all works at a frantic pace – the stages all have two sets of instruments so as to keep the momentum going – as one act performs, one is packing up and leaving the stage and the next act is already setting up.

'I was like, "Holy s***!" Am I going to survive this?' Katy told reporter Sheryl Garratt during the tour. 'Because I know bands that come back and they're just exhausted afterwards. There's none of the props and production values I'll have in the future. There's no sound-check, you just set up, play your

set and get the hell off. I'm usually following the last screamo hardcore punk band, facing this sea of black hoodies, and I'm in this little dress and trying to jump off the monitors like the boys. See, I have a Les Paul guitar [like them], too – but it's f***ing bubblegum-pink!'

After each gig, she and her band packed up and headed for the tour-buses – often for a journey of a few hundred miles to the next car park in the next town where they were due to play. 'They're saying this is the worst tour I'll ever do,' she continued. 'I may be a pop girl, but I'm surviving Warped. And I don't think many of them bitches could!'

It probably helped that she knew some people on the tour – namely her boyfriend's band Gym Class Heroes. Katy didn't want anyone thinking she was a girl tagging along with Travis, though. 'I'm not a needy girl; we Hudsons are very independent!' she said at the time. She did, however, allow him to carry her onto the stage for some of her performances. 'I was voted "laziest" by everybody on the tour!' she added, proudly.

While Katy spent the summer on sweaty buses with other bands, the success of 'I Kissed a Girl' went global, and she noticed her name and face were being recognised. 'The other day I was in Canada,' she told reporter Tim Nixon on the tour. 'I was grabbing some food with my band at this restaurant. I noticed the waiters had this quote on the back of their shirts and the quote said "I've kissed more girls than Katy Perry". It was the most random thing I've ever seen in my life! I was like: "What's happening? Who did this? Is this a joke? Am I being Punk'd right now?" When I see little things like that, I think: "What did I do?"'

There was also lots of speculation in the press about whether Katy had actually kissed a girl herself. In some interviews she would say no, but in others she would coyly suggest she had. When asked by *The Times*' Sophie Harris in August 2008, Katy replied 'Oh yes, it was delightful', and she described herself as 'metrosexual' when quizzed about her sexuality. Travis was never far away, however (he was in the next room during Harris's interview, lying on the bed waiting for Katy), and he even hung around with Katy's parents during the tour. While Katy would not be drawn in interviews about how serious the relationship was ('We don't know what's in the cards. But we're holding the cards and we're gonna play 'em'), she did give Travis, who is an experienced tattoo artist as well as a hip hop star, permission to tattoo her own dad, Keith. 'My dad wants to get a tattoo from him,' Katy revealed at the time. 'Dad's got three tattoos already. They all say "Jesus".'

Despite Travis's presence, the press kept guessing, and Katy fuelled the fire herself at a concert in George, Washington during the Warped Tour. On 9 August, she pulled a girl up onto the stage and kissed her, and the kiss was soon posted on YouTube for everyone (including Katy's horrified parents, and Travis) to see. The sixteen-year-old who Katy kissed was named Jenna Buhmann, and she not only kissed *the* girl, she didn't mind the sudden press attention she got afterwards either (if you watch the clip, it does look like she burst into tears of happiness, though).

Buhmann told the *Daily Mirror*: 'I was quite near the front and had my arms reached out towards [Katy], singing along. She looked me right in the eyes for about fifteen seconds, and that's when I knew it was going to happen. I puckered up my lips, she let go of the bodyguard's arm, grabbed my arm and pulled me towards her. I grabbed her face, put my hand on the back of her head and just kissed her. The crowd went crazy.'

So what did Jenna think of her kiss with Katy? 'It was so exhilarating, it was such a rush. She was a good kisser and she had very soft lips. The kiss didn't last that long, but to me it felt like it lasted forever. She's a pretty attractive, sexy lady.' To begin with, Jenna's friends and family didn't even believe her when she said what had happened, and it was only when they saw the YouTube clip that they saw for themselves that it was true.

As soon as the Warped Tour finished, Katy had more promotional duties to attend to. While the album *One of the Boys* had been released in the USA, it was yet to be released worldwide, so Capitol Records decided that now was the time for Katy to board a plane bound for Europe and let fans on the other side of the Atlantic get to know her better. With a UK release date for the album scheduled for 22 September, Katy headed off for another round of interviews, live performances and TV appearances to cement her success worldwide.

One of her first discoveries when she arrived in England was that she was perceived differently in the UK from how she was seen in America. 'Wherever I go in Europe, it seems people understand and get the joke more,' she said of her songs and pop persona. Brits, it seemed, understood her fun brand of confessional pop humour, whether she was singing about kissing a girl ('The British have a warped sense of humour, just like I do') or 'Waking Up in Vegas', worrying she has done a Britney Spears and got married after a drunken weekend.

The mini-tour of Europe was jam-packed, taking place in late August and September and covering numerous cities. In an interview with Poppy Cosyns, Katy recounted the schedule: 'This morning I was in Milan and a couple of mornings before that I was in Germany and London and Paris. I'm zig-zagging all over Europe, then for like seventeen days, I'm in Australia, New Mexico and Japan. It's incredibly hectic but there are no complaints. The perks are f***ing amazing and I'm doing what I always wanted to do.'

Among the dates was a sold-out show at the Scala in London, with singer Adele as Katy's special musical guest. It was a great venue for Katy to play, steeped in entertainment and rock history. Originally a cinema, the Scala sits near King's Cross station and was opened in 1920. Damaged during the Blitz, it was closed until 1952, when it reopened, refurbished, as the Gaumont Cinema. It was renamed an Odeon in 1970, and by 1971 had gained a reputation for showing adult movies. It also became an all-night music venue at this time, with artists including Iggy Pop performing to sell-out crowds.

Unfortunately the Scala's late-night licence was revoked in 1974, following a petition by local residents, and soon after it closed. It re-opened as the Scala Cinema in 1981 – and was known for showing movies such as the controversial *A Clockwork Orange* – before finally becoming a bona fide rock venue in 1999 after a major refit. Acts who have played there include Adam Ant, The Libertines, Coldplay, Sheryl Crow and the Chemical Brothers.

It was a perfect venue for Katy, and the addition of Adele was a good match as the pair had much in common – Adele, like Katy, had started singing as a child (Adele in the less sunny surroundings of Tottenham in London), and gained fans on the internet before she ever had a record deal. Just twenty years old when she and Katy played the Scala, the singer-songwriter's best-known hit to date was 'Chasing Pavements'. They wowed the crowds.

Meanwhile, as Katy was zipping from country to country, she was also being nominated for awards for her first number one, 'I Kissed a Girl'. On 7 September, she briefly arrived back in the USA to appear at the MTV Video Music Awards 2008, presented by British comedian Russell Brand at the Paramount Studios lot in Los Angeles. It was a dream come true for the young singer ('It was awesome. This is a TV show that I would sneak away to my friend's house to watch. To think they would even give me a good seat was like, "Come on!"').

Katy was nominated in five categories: Best Female Video, Best New Artist, Best Art Direction, Best Editing and Best Cinematography, but unfortunately she didn't go home with any prizes. The Best Female Video award went to Britney Spears for 'Piece of Me', while Best New Artist went to Tokyo Hotel for their song 'Ready Set Go'. Katy did, however, get to meet Brand, and he asked her – along with pop stars Christina Aguilera and Pink – if she would appear in his upcoming movie *Get Him to the Greek* that was going to be filmed mainly in 2009.

Russell got all three of them to agree and then filmed a scene in which he kissed Katy (and another in which he kissed Pink!) to be used in the movie. 'In the scenes with Pink and Katy Perry, I had to do kissing,' Brand boasted to the *Sun*. 'I got to snog them both in a day. Katy Perry is lovely, she is the kind of girl who would skip down stairs lightly. And Pink is a lovely woman – a forceful, sexy woman. With both of them I didn't act, the acting stopped.'

When Katy was asked what she thought of Russell, she answered: 'He's hot in person. I appreciate his kind of f***ed up sense of humour, he's hilarious.'

Little did Russell or Katy know that their paths would cross again with much more meaning one year later. Instead, Katy went home to boyfriend Travis after filming the scene, and Russell returned to his LA hotel where his Australian girlfriend, Teresa Palmer, was waiting.

By now, the reviews for Katy's album were coming in from all over the world. Critics were divided about *One of the Boys*, with its ironic lyrics and poppy songs. Everyone speculated on how autobiographical the songs were – Katy had admitted she had kissed a girl, so did that mean the other songs were true, too? Certainly all of the songs, each co-written by Katy, had stories to tell. As well as 'I Kissed a Girl', 'Waking Up in Vegas' and 'Ur So Gay', the album included:

★ 'Thinking of You' – a break-up song in which she is thinking about a previous love when she kisses her current guy
★ 'Mannequin' – a song about being in love with someone with no heart
★ 'If You Can Afford Me' – in which she sings about being

high-maintenance, and never being a one-night stand
★ 'Hot n Cold' – Katy sings about a boy who changes his mind all the time
★ 'Lost' – a song about being lost and alone and hung-over, surrounded by fair-weather friends (reviewers speculated that this might be Katy singing about her life in LA, away from her family)
★ 'Self Inflicted' – another song about being in love with someone who may not be good for her
★ 'One of the Boys' – Katy sings about being seen as one of the boys when she wants one man to see her as a girl ('I wanna be a flower, not a dirty weed / And I wanna smell like roses, not a baseball team')
★ 'Fingerprints' – a song about wanting to make an impression and not be just another face in the crowd. ('I wanted to end [the album] with "Fingerprints", which is basically a way of leaving my mark,' says Katy.)

She admitted in interviews that many of the songs were autobiographical: 'I can almost give you a person that they're about, not that I should,' she said to one interviewer. 'I have different ex-boyfriends represented and friends and bits of my life are all as an open book.' Katy also told the *Scotsman* reporter Gary Graff that she was not just your average girl pop star, either. 'I think sometimes people are just surprised there is a girl in pop music that's just saying it like it is, because you're so used to these more controlled pop girls and Disney people,' she said at the time. 'I think that, being a songwriter, you've got to tell good stories, and I tell all the colours of the rainbow, not just the pink ones.'

Fans loved the album, and some of the critics raved about it, too. The *New York Post* said 'Music sensation Katy Perry is exploding like a supernova', while influential music bible *Billboard* said that 'not since [Alanis Morissette's] *Jagged Little Pill* has a debut album been so packed with potential hits'. Meanwhile, the UK's *Q* magazine nominated 'I Kissed a Girl' as their best track of the year. Not every review was positive, of course. Stephen Erlewine of allmusic.com called Katy a 'trollop singing with the desperation of a fading burlesque star twice her age' and called the album 'a grotesque emblem of all the wretched excesses of this decade', while British music magazine *NME* found it 'beyond comprehension' how 'this crap can be battery-fed to the nation's young when there's pop artists as thrilling as Ladyhawke recording today'.

Harsh words, but Katy took them all in her stride. After all, the sales spoke for themselves – even if critics didn't always like the album, there were plenty of people who did. The album sold 47,000 copies in its first week in the USA, and has since sold well over a million copies there. It has also been certified as a platinum-selling release in the UK, Australia and Canada.

Katy didn't have much time to enjoy her success. After the faster-than-light mini-tour of Europe, and her trip to the MTV VMAs, Katy was back giving interviews and making appearances to promote the 30 September release of the album's next single, 'Hot n Cold', which had already entered the *Billboard* US charts as a result of digital downloads, before any CDs of the song had been pressed. 'I'm just so happy with it because it represents a broader perspective of who I am, not just the cute, sexy little kitten Katy,' she remarked when the song was released. The song, with its catchy refrain ('You're hot then you're cold, you're yes then you're no, you're in and you're out . . . ') was another personal one for Katy.

'It's about a very real relationship,' she told journalist Tim Nixon. 'I was with this boy I really, really cared for and we'd been having a conversation by text or by email and then he'd just disappear. For like three days! It would drive me crazy 'cause I'd be like "Where'd you go? I thought we were making plans for this weekend?" I realised this guy was the moodiest motherf***er I ever met and honestly that's all it came down to. He changed moods like he was going through the menopause.'

While some speculated that the song was about her current beau, Travis, Katy refused to be drawn. The pair was often photographed out and about and happy, with Travis proclaiming his love for Katy by buying her a promise ring. 'I went in [to the jewellers] and said I wanted a ring,' he told *People* magazine. 'The lady behind the counter said "Here's one for $300". I was like "I want a *nice* ring!" Then I pointed to the big one.'

Katy wore the ring on her middle left finger (one over from her wedding finger) and Travis got himself a silver band to wear, with 'Katy' engraved on it. He was nervous about giving it to her but 'she was so excited! And I had set up flowers everywhere.' The two – he with his popular band, Gym Class Heroes, her with a number one single to her name – were soon being declared music's current power couple in the press.

In between the romance and interviews, Katy headed off to film a music video to accompany the 'Hot n Cold' single release. The song had been written by Katy, Dr Luke (who had also co-written 'I Kissed a Girl' with Katy) and Max Martin (who wrote Britney Spears' massive first hit, '... Baby One More Time'), and the video was to be directed by Alan Ferguson, a video director who had worked with Gym Class Heroes (including on their video 'Cupid's Chokehold', which Katy had appeared in), Natasha Bedingfield and Fall Out Boy.

The video told a story, beginning with bride Katy and groom 'Alexander' (played by model/actor Alexander Rodriguez, a friend of Katy's) standing at the altar. It's his turn to say 'I do', but as the music begins he makes a run for it, out of the church, and Katy follows in hot pursuit. The video then has her chasing him down the street, on foot and by bike, still in her wedding dress, and sometimes accompanied by bridesmaids carrying baseball bats! At the end, when she finally catches up with him, we see that Alexander is actually still in the church and was dreaming the whole thing. The video ends when he answers the question, 'Do you take this woman ... ' with the reply, 'I do', and then he and Katy dash out of the church as a happily married couple. Aww.

It's a fun video to match a catchy song. Soon you couldn't turn on a radio anywhere in the world without hearing it, and 'Hot n Cold' raced up the charts in the USA, the UK, Canada, Australia and much of Europe. Because of some of the language used in the song (Katy sings 'You PMS like a bitch, I would know'), various edits of the song had to be released for radio and TV that either cut out the word 'bitch' altogether or substituted it with 'chick' or 'girl'. But even that hiccup couldn't stop its rise in the charts, and soon the song was so popular that producers were lining up to use it in TV shows and film soundtracks. Just a few of the places where the song is featured include the romantic comedy *The Ugly Truth* with Gerard Butler and Katherine Heigl, the trailer for the Sandra Bullock and Ryan Reynolds movie *The Proposal*, the *American Pie* sequel *American Pie Presents: The Book of Love*, the TV series *90210* (the twenty-first-century update of *Beverly Hills 90210*), the fantasy drama series *Ghost Whisperer*, and the family movie *Alvin and the Chipmunks: The Squeakquel* (in which some of the chipmunk girls sing the song in their squeaky voices).

Katy even recorded the song in the fabricated language Simlish, for the soundtrack of the role-playing computer game Sims 2: Apartment Life. And 'Hot n Cold' was such a hit that other artists decided to record their own versions, too, including ska band Kid British, and metalcore band Woe, Is Me.

By the time 2008 was nearing its end, it seemed Katy was no longer just a new pop princess. With cover versions aplenty and non-stop airplay of her songs, she was now a pop queen, but there was also a rival to her throne emerging . . .

6

Pop Queen

As 2008 was drawing to a close, Katy was increasingly busy promoting her album *One of the Boys*. Now hugely popular in Europe as well in as the United States, she was asked not only to perform, but also to present the MTV Europe Music Awards – and she was nominated for two awards, too.

The MTV Europe Music Awards have been held since 1994, and they celebrate the most popular music videos in Europe. A European companion to MTV's Video Music Awards in the USA, the awards are voted for by viewers of all the different regional channels that make up MTV Europe. Each year, a different country hosts the awards, with the first ceremony held in Berlin, by the famous Brandenburg Gate. And each year, there is a different celebrity host – beginning with Tom Jones in 1994. Since then, the famous people who have taken on the nerve-wracking role of emcee for the evening include Robbie Williams, Ronan Keating, Christina Aguilera, Borat (a.k.a. Sacha Baron Cohen), Snoop Dogg and Justin Timberlake.

It was quite an honour for a relatively new star like Katy

to be asked to present the 2008 awards in Liverpool. While not as well known as its American counterpart, the awards show has seen some memorable moments over the years, from George Michael performing 'Freedom' accompanied by well-known supermodels, to Marilyn Manson singing 'Rock is Dead' while wearing nothing more than a G-string.

'I've never done it before, so I hope it works,' Katy told reporters at a press conference before the show, when asked how she was feeling about presenting the awards. She certainly didn't look nervous at the prospect of appearing live on TV, in front of millions of viewers.

Katy, of course, was bound to make her own unique mark on the show. The awards ceremony opened in spectacularly kooky style, with her performing her mega-hit 'I Kissed a Girl', singing the song as only she could, wearing an American football outfit and straddling a gigantic cherry chap-stick in reference to the song's lyrics. (She even commented, 'I must say I've seen bigger – hi baby!' while looking at the chap-stick and then her boyfriend Travis, who was in the audience.) Over the course of the evening she managed an impressive twelve costume changes as she introduced presenters such as Grace Jones, Bono, Leona Lewis and Travis McCoy, and watched acts including Take That, Beyoncé, The Killers and Pink perform live. Among the outfits were a striking blue dress from Jean-Charles de Castelbajac, on which eyes and eyelashes adorned the bust, a yellow dress with President Obama's face on it, a chiffon dress she wore while being lowered onto stage on a giant banana, and a multicoloured dress with a skirt that became a carousel, complete with miniature horses.

It was an evening that was as fun as Katy's clothes, with awards given out to Britney Spears (Best Act of 2008, Album of the Year), Kanye West (Ultimate Urban), Tokio Hotel (Best Headliner) and Sir Paul McCartney, who won the Ultimate Legend Award. It was appropriate that the awards were held in Liverpool, where he and George Harrison, Ringo Starr and John Lennon formed The Beatles, and he was genuinely pleased with his prize. 'Many years ago, four little boys were born here in Liverpool and we went on to do quite well,' he said at the ceremony. 'So thanks to all my family, to all of you for coming along, everyone in Liverpool, everyone in Britain, everyone in America – for voting in Mr Obama. I love you!'

There was a surprise winner that evening, too. One of the awards was for Best Act Ever, and U2, Britney Spears and Green Day were among the nominees. More surprisingly, Eighties pop star Rick Astley was also nominated, following the craze that summer that was called 'Rickrolling', in which web users unwittingly ended up being linked to clips of his best-known single, 'Never Gonna Give You Up'. This phe-nomenon led to an online campaign to orchestrate votes, leading to Mr Astley – surely relatively unknown outside the UK – winning the title Best Act Ever!

Katy finished the show as memorably as she began it, performing 'Hot n Cold', in an outfit that was half tux-edo, half wedding dress. She didn't go home empty-handed, either. She was nominated in two categories, Most Addictive Track (for 'I Kissed a Girl') and Best New Act. While she lost the Most Addictive Track award to Pink's 'So What', she won Best New Act and received it in typical Katy style: 'It's a fix! I demand a recount!!'

Not everything was going so well for her, unfortunately. Despite her obvious affection for boyfriend Travis during the awards, the couple now found themselves on rocky ground. They travelled to Mexico a few weeks later for the Christmas holidays, but it wasn't a romantic vacation, more a last-ditch attempt to save their relationship, which had suffered from them rarely being in the same place at the same time while both of their music careers took off.

Returning from the make-or-break trip, Travis took to his blog on friendsorenemies.com to announce their split. He posted some lyrics on the blog from the hip hop song 'Looking at the Front Door' by Main Source. The song includes the lyrics 'We fight every night, now that's not kosher / I reminisce with bliss of when we was closer / And wake up to be greeted by an argument again / You act like you're ten.'

He also declared his new relationship was with his more reliable laptop: 'My laptop is my new bitch. LOYAL. LISTENS. And NEVER LETS ME DOWN.'

To begin with, Katy wouldn't comment on the end of her relationship with Travis. Eventually, she did say something when asked about the break-up by *Time Out Chicago*. The magazine noted that, just before their split, Travis had two new, rather unusual, tattoos on his hands – portraits of Seventies/Eighties soul group Hall & Oates! Could that be the reason Katy ended it?

'Not at all,' she laughed at the time. 'It's actually bonus points – Hall & Oates are the best group ever!' On stage in Los Angeles, at the Hotel Café a few weeks later, Katy did reveal a little more: 'It hurts right now. When you break up with someone, you move on. You don't want to move on but you have to because they don't give you any choice. But I'm over it!' By the end of January, though, she was even joking about any rumours of romance that may follow her break-up. 'I've actually taken a vow of celibacy this year – no kissing anyone. Just my cat, Kitty Purry.'

While her relationship with Travis was over and played out in the press, Katy also had to deal with negative stories appearing in the papers that seemed to set her against British pop star Lily Allen. The 'feud', as the press called it, began in December 2008.

First, Katy made the mistake of describing herself in an interview as a 'fatter version of Amy Winehouse and the skinnier version of Lily Allen'. She did apologise, however, telling Usmagazine.com that the comment had been made in jest: 'I was just kind of joking and trying to be funny. I didn't mean anything by it. Comedians are not necessarily meant to be taken super-seriously.'

Lily didn't accept Katy's apology. On 8 December 2008, she was being interviewed on Capital FM radio in London when she launched a scathing attack on her pop rival. 'I happen to know for a fact that she was an American version of *me*,' Lily said on air. 'She was signed by my label in America as "We need to find something controversial and kooky like Lily Allen". And then they found her. I think the lyrics and stuff are a bit crass. It's like, you're not English and you don't write your own songs, shut up!' Lily was mistaken, of course, as Katy had written or co-written all the tracks on *One of the Boys*, but the battle lines were drawn between the pair nonetheless.

Katy wasn't the first person Lily had publicly fallen out with. The outspoken star had courted controversy from the moment she rose to fame. The daughter of actor Keith Allen and film producer Alison Owen, Lily had a quirky upbringing before she became a star – she appeared on TV for the first time when she was just three years old, in a small role in *The Comic Strip Presents*, alongside her dad. Keith left the family home by the time Lily was four, and while she grew up in a council house she also attended some of the best public schools, thirteen of them in all, including Bedales and Hill House, which lists Prince Charles amongst its former pupils. She also counted comedian Harry Enfield (who dated her mother) and The Clash's Joe Strummer as family friends – not something many children could boast.

Lily was often in trouble at school, which is not surprising when you learn she was smoking dope and taking ecstasy in her early teens, and she was expelled more than once for drinking and smoking. Dropping out of education for good when she was fifteen, she ended up in Ibiza, working in a record store and dealing ecstasy to make a living. It was there that she met her first manager, George Lamb. After being rejected by several record labels, Lily was signed to London Records in 2002, but she was later dropped and the folk album she had recorded (with songs written by her dad) was never released. After more failed attempts at getting a record made, Lily posted some demos of her songs on her MySpace page in 2005, and the buzz about her began to grow. In 2006, the press started to become interested, and – five years after she began her musical career – Lily found

herself with a record deal at last and a debut single ('Smile')
climbing the charts.

Lily, it seems, has a lot in common with Katy in her
struggle to get to the top, but it certainly didn't make them
friends. Katy wasn't the only one to feel Lily's anger, however.
Before she attacked Katy in the press, Lily had been known
for her controversial, outspoken ways towards other stars.
In 2007, she raised her glass to troubled Amy Winehouse
(who had entered rehab the week before) on stage at the V
Festival, and shouted, 'You have got to have a drink. Here's
to Amy Winehouse . . . ha!' She then introduced the song
'Everything's Just Wonderful' by saying 'All these skinny girls
in the magazines, "Look at me, look at me!" – heroin addicts!
You are not that skinny unless you have an eating disorder
or a drug habit,' which the press translated as a thinly veiled
insult to Winehouse.

Kylie Minogue was also a target of Lily's acid tongue.
Lily wasn't impressed that Kylie was booked to play the
Glastonbury Festival in 2007, and she made her feelings
known. 'To me, Kylie playing Glastonbury would be the ultimate insult to it. It should be about new, interesting music,
not mainstream pop.'

Even music legend Sir Elton John incurred her wrath. At
the *GQ* Men of the Year awards in September 2008, the pair
presented the show together but when Elton joked about
Lily's drinking, she replied in front of the entire audience:
'F*** off Elton. I'm forty years younger than you and I have
my whole life ahead of me.' The pair simmered at each other
for a year, until they finally made up in late 2009.

Lily's feud with Katy lasted quite a while, too. By March

2009, Katy had defended her comments once again in the press, telling *Heat* magazine: 'I really didn't mean to upset her. What I actually said was that I was a skinnier version of Lily and a fatter version of Amy Winehouse. But Lily is skinny now. She is hot – she looks really good.'

Her comments didn't calm Lily down. As 2009 began, Lily posted on her Facebook page that she knew Katy's mobile phone number. 'I'm just waiting for her to open her mouth one more time then it hits Facebook,' she wrote. Katy didn't rise to the bait; instead, she took to the press to say something nice about Lily instead.

'I love Lily. She's great. I bought her record. It's a game in the industry to kind of plant things, and most of the time people have nothing to do with them,' she told James Montgomery at MTV. Over the next few months, the 'feud' disappeared from the newspapers. Anyway, Katy had much more on her mind than a tabloid-fuelled tiff, or even the break-up with Travis. At the MTV Europe Awards, she had announced she would go on tour in the New Year, her first as a solo performer, and she also had a new single to release, 'Thinking of You'. Life was getting even more hectic.

First on Katy's list of things to do in 2009 was the release of the fourth single from her album, called 'Thinking of You'. Written by Katy, it was produced by Butch Walker, a friend of Katy's fellow female pop/rock star Pink.

Katy had originally made a do-it-yourself video for the song with friends back in 2007, that was available to watch on YouTube in 2008, but in December 2008 she filmed an official video to tie in with the single's 12 January release. It was another music video that told a story – but this time it was a more sombre one than those in her previous hits. In the video, Katy plays a woman in the 1940s, during the Second World War, who gets up from her bed, where her boyfriend (model Anderson Davis) lies, clearly thinking about someone else. She pins a picture of a man in uniform (Matt Dallas, best known for his leading role in the series *Kyle XY*) to her mirror as she sings 'When I'm with him I am thinking of you'. It flashes back to their romance and happier times, and to when he went away to war. Then as Katy lies with her new man, we see that her true love died on the battlefield. The video ends after she reads the telegram telling her of his death, with her getting dressed in black to go to his funeral. Sad stuff indeed, and while the song didn't have the chart success of Katy's previous hits, the video was viewed over five million times on YouTube. It was directed by Melina, who had also directed videos for Rihanna's song 'Rude Boy', Leona Lewis's 'Bleeding Love', Beyoncé's 'Diva' and Kylie Minogue's 'In My Arms'.

As soon as the song was released, it was time for Katy to hit the road. She kicked off her first live tour, the appropriately named Hello Katy tour, on 23 January 2009. She had announced the dates shortly after the MTV Europe Awards and tickets soon sold out. The tour started in Seattle, and Katy got to play some famous concert halls, including the Fillmore in San Francisco, one of America's most historic music venues. The Grateful Dead, The Doors, Jimi Hendrix, The Who, Aretha Franklin and Miles Davis all played there in the 1960s, and when the Fillmore reopened after a refurbishment in the 1990s following damage in an earthquake, the Smashing Pumpkins was the first band to walk across the famous stage.

After performing at such a prestigious venue, Katy hopped over to Europe to spend February performing sell-out concerts in Germany, Sweden, Denmark, London (where she performed at Camden nightclub Koko), Paris and Belgium.

Then it was back to America in March for more dates there, which continued into April and May. Katy followed these with shows in Japan, and by June she was back in Europe again, this time playing bigger venues including the Shepherd's Bush Empire in London, L'Olympia in Paris and the Palacio de Deportes in Madrid. The tour also encompassed performances at some of Europe's best-known festivals, including Scotland's T in the Park and England's V Festival.

It was a punishing schedule, but Katy loved every moment – especially the chance to play in her old home town, Santa Barbara, in August 2009. At each venue, her setlist remained pretty much the same – as well as including her hits 'Hot n Cold' and 'Thinking of You' and tracks from *One of the Boys*, Katy also performed a cover version of The Outfield's song 'Use Your Love' and, as an encore along with 'I Kissed a Girl', she sang Queen's 'Don't Stop Me Now'.

In between all the tour dates, Katy didn't have time to rest. February is awards-time in the music industry, and there were two important dates in her diary, the Grammy Awards on 8 February and the Brit Awards ten days later. First, Katy got on a plane bound for Los Angeles to attend the fifty-first Grammy Awards, which were to be held at the mega-arena Staples Center – a huge venue that would be host to the Michael Jackson memorial later in the year.

The Grammys (originally known as the Gramophone Awards when they were launched in 1958) are the Oscars of the music world, so it was a very important night for Katy. Since 1971, they have been broadcast around the world on TV, and the artists who have picked up one of the distinctive gramophone-shaped awards include Frank Sinatra, Stevie Wonder, The Beatles, U2, George Michael, Fleetwood Mac, Alanis Morissette and Michael Jackson.

Katy was asked to perform 'I Kissed a Girl' at the awards, and she joined an impressive line-up of acts on stage that night. There was U2, Coldplay with Jay-Z, Stevie Wonder, Paul McCartney with Dave Grohl of the Foo Fighters, Neil Diamond, Justin Timberlake and Adele. Of course, Katy made another distinctive entrance. She was lowered in a vertical banana onto a giant-fruit-covered stage, wearing a corset dress adorned with what was, presumably, her five-a-day allowance of fruit. She danced on stage with a group of white tuxedo-wearing female dancers, who later ripped off their jackets to reveal sparkly bra tops, while in the background, picture frames showed images of members of the public singing along to her song.

As she said on the red carpet following the awards: 'When I was growing up, imagining myself at the Grammy Awards, I don't think I imagined I would be riding a giant banana into a fruit bowl!' It was certainly memorable.

In between the performances, the awards were given out. Adele, whom Katy had performed with in London, was up for Record of the Year for 'Chasing Pavements', but was beaten by Robert Plant and Alison Krauss's duet 'Please Read the Letter'. They also won Album of the Year. Adele did win Best New Artist and also Best Female Pop Vocal Performance, an award Katy had been nominated for.

It was a great night nonetheless. Katy got to meet some of the singers and songwriters she had always admired, and if people hadn't known who Katy Perry was before the Grammy Awards, they certainly knew by the end of the evening, following her show-stopping performance.

Unfortunately, the press coverage of the Grammys that year was not focused on the awards ceremony itself. R&B singer Rihanna – who would soon become one of Katy's best friends – had been due to perform at the awards with her boyfriend, singer Chris Brown. Their performance was cancelled only hours before the ceremony was due to begin and no one knew why. However, reports filtered through on the morning after the Grammys that Chris had handed himself into Los Angeles police, following an alleged assault on a woman believed to be Rihanna. Apparently, police had been called the night before – following an argument between the couple in their car – and he was arrested. Within days, photos emerged of the damage he had inflicted to Rihanna's face, and all thoughts of the awards ceremony itself were forgotten. (By early March, Chris had been charged with assault and making criminal threats; he later received a five-year probation for the crime.)

Katy, meanwhile, had another important date to make. Ten days after the Grammy Awards came the UK equivalent, the Brit Awards, so she hopped onto another plane to fly to England.

Established in 1977, the awards were originally known as the BPI Awards, but were renamed the Brits in 1989. Televised in Britain since the 1980s, the show was broadcast live until the infamous awards in 1989, presented by Samantha Fox and Mick Fleetwood. Badly organised and seemingly unrehearsed, the show was a disaster and has gone down in history for its awfulness. What could go wrong, did – Fox and Fleetwood had never presented an award show before and often got their scripted lines mixed up, while the autocue was also faulty. They announced the Four Tops were next on stage but Boy George appeared instead, and an acceptance video from Michael Jackson was never shown at all.

From then on, the show was recorded so that any goofs or swearing on behalf of the assembled rock stars could be edited out before broadcast. That didn't mean that the slightly raucous, rebellious vibe of the show was lost, however. Three years later, in 1992, The KLF performed a death-metal version of '3 a.m. Eternal' that so offended Hungarian composer Sir George Solti that he left the awards and had to be persuaded to return. The KLF then left the building and, when they won an award, sent a motorcycle courier to collect it from the stage (the producers wouldn't allow this, however).

The show was also infamous for Pulp singer Jarvis Cocker's antics in 1996, when he leapt up on stage while Michael Jackson performed 'Earth Song'. Offended that Jackson's performance involved him standing Christ-like while singing, surrounded by adoring kiddies, Cocker ran across the stage and then waved his bottom at the audience.

And who could forget Danbert Nobacon of political

band Chumbawamba throwing a bucket of iced water over Labour politician John Prescott?; Mel C (in 1997) and Robbie Williams (in 2000) both challenging Liam Gallagher to fights, following his comments about them?; Geri Halliwell's infamous Union Jack dress, which she wore when the Spice Girls performed in 1997?; or DJ Brandon Block's drunken stagger on stage and subsequent slanging match with Rolling Stones guitarist Ronnie Wood? Yes, the Brits have always been the most memorable awards in the music calendar.

The 2009 Brit Awards, held at Earls Court in London on 18 February 2009 was surprisingly sedate in comparison with previous years. Hosted by *Gavin & Stacey* stars James Corden and Matthew Horne, alongside pop star Kylie Minogue, the show was promoted as being broadcast live but there was actually a small time delay, just in case anyone said a rude word or decided to storm the stage as had happened before. There were some great acts performing in between the awards themselves – U2, Kylie Minogue, Girls Aloud, Coldplay, Duffy, the re-formed Take That, and, because they were receiving the award for Outstanding Contribution to Music, the Pet Shop Boys finished the show. Katy was nominated for the Best International Female Award, and she won.

A very croaky Katy, who was coming down with flu, went up to the stage – in a black leotard decorated with Hello Kitty jewellery – to accept the award from Lionel Richie. 'I just want to thank everybody here in London and in the UK. I am so sick right now but they said I should show up to the Brits because something special might happen, so thank you so much!'

By the next morning there were rumours that Katy's

sickness had developed as the evening went on, with NME. com reporting that she threw up backstage shortly after accepting the award and then had to head back to her hotel. Celebrity blogger Perez Hilton confirmed what happened. 'Just got a text from Katy. She had to leave the Brits after she won. She's so sick that she puked backstage! "Very punk rock," she says!' (There were even rumours that she had actually thrown up onto Lionel Richie, but this was untrue – 'I threw up a little bit in my mouth,' she told *Time Out Chicago*. 'I didn't throw up a lot, which everybody was saying. I desperately needed to go home. Lionel Richie presented me my award – but no, I did not throw up on him at all!')

Because Katy left before the end of the show, she missed a performance that she would have found very interesting. The Pet Shop Boys performed a ten-minute finale to mark their lifetime award and were joined halfway through by the woman who was threatening to steal Katy's pop crown – an American singer named Lady Gaga.

While Katy Perry had been building her own career in California, a young woman named Stefani Joanne Angelina Germanotta had been doing the same on the East Coast of America. Born in New York City in 1986 (she's eighteen months younger than Katy), Stefani, like Katy, was singing from an early age. She began to learn to play the piano at the age of four, and by thirteen had written her first ballad.

Stefani, like Katy, had a religious upbringing (her family are Italian-American Catholics) and she attended the same private Manhattan Roman Catholic school as Paris Hilton, Convent of the Sacred Heart, often appearing in the school's musical productions, playing Adelaide in *Guys and Dolls* and

Philia in *A Funny Thing Happened on the Way to the Forum*. Already quite an outgoing person with her own quirky sense of style, she told *InTouch* magazine that she didn't fit in at school with her fellow pupils: 'I was a bit insecure in high school. I used to get made fun of for being either too provocative or too eccentric, so I started to tone it down. I didn't fit in, and I felt like a freak.'

When she was seventeen, Stefani became one of a very select few when she was granted early admission to New York University's prestigious Tisch School of the Arts, where she studied music and concentrated on her songwriting. After a year-and-a-half, she decided to drop out of college to concentrate on her music career. Like Katy, she was determined to succeed, and she convinced her father to pay her rent for a year while she tried to make it big – if she failed, she promised to return to school. 'I left my entire family, got the cheapest apartment I could find, and ate s*** until somebody would listen,' she told *New York* magazine. So, just like a certain West Coast singer, Stefani was still a teenager, but living away from her family and trying to make it on her own.

She also had a few failed attempts at getting a record deal, just like Katy did. A deal with Def Jam Records fell through after just a few months. She performed in clubs on the Lower East Side, gaining a reputation for delivering her songs on stage in a way that was almost performance art, and she travelled to New Jersey to work with record producer Rob Fusari, who helped her write some of her earliest songs.

Rob helped in another way. One of Stefani's major influences (again, something she shares with Katy) was the rock band Queen. As Rob told the *Star Ledger* newspaper: 'Every day, when Stef came to the studio, instead of saying hello, I would start singing "Radio Ga Ga". That was her entrance song,' he remembers. Stefani was trying to come up with a stage name when she received a text from him one day that said 'Lady Gaga'. 'It was actually a glitch,' says Fusari. 'I typed "Radio Ga Ga" in a text and it did an autocorrect so somehow "Radio" got changed to "Lady". She texted me back, "That's it." After that day, she was Lady Gaga. She's like, "Don't ever call me Stefani again."'

And so, in 2006, Lady Gaga was born. (There has been some debate about whether Rob Fusari's story is true, with the *NY Post* suggesting the name was thought up in a marketing meeting, but Fusari's story is more fun.) She began collaborating with performance artist Lady Starlight in 2007, performing The Ultimate Pop Burlesque Rock Show in venues in downtown Manhattan. Dressed in raunchy corset-style clothes, Lady Gaga began to weave into her music sounds that paid homage to the Seventies styles of David Bowie and Queen, and the buzz about her began to grow.

She was signed to Streamline Records, part of Interscope, later that year, around the time Katy was between record deals. Lady Gaga was also hired to write songs for other people including Fergie of the Black Eyed Peas, Britney Spears, the Pussycat Dolls and New Kids on the Block. 'Getting into writing for others happened naturally, because at the time, I didn't have a record deal,' Gaga told *Billboard* magazine. 'I don't have an ego about other people singing my songs.'

While Katy was securing her record deal with Capitol, Lady Gaga was signing her own contracts in New York, and then relocating to Los Angeles to work on her debut album, which was to be called *The Fame*. Released in August 2008, just as Katy's 'I Kissed a Girl' was topping the charts worldwide and her album *One of the Boys* was flying off the shelves, Lady Gaga's *The Fame* contained her first, huge hit, 'Just Dance', which topped the charts in Australia, Canada, the UK and the USA. Gaga followed this with the even-more-successful single, 'Poker Face', and by the end of 2008, her face and her unique dress sense were known around the globe.

Like Katy, Lady Gaga's style has gained her as much press comment as her music. However, while Katy's dress sense – which often harks back to the Fifties and Sixties, with high-waisted shorts and halter-tops – is fun and flirty, Lady Gaga's is more outlandish and often extremely revealing. As 2009 began, Gaga became known for a series of bizarre outfits, including the 'bubble dress' (a dress made out of some very strategically placed plastic bubbles) she wore on the cover of *Rolling Stone* magazine, and one made out of Kermit the Frog muppets. She also described herself as 'a walking piece of art' with her bleach-blonde hair (which she reportedly dyed from her natural dark brown as people often thought she was Amy Winehouse) and quirky outfits.

As the year continued, Katy and Lady Gaga seemed to take turns being in the press for their outfits, their music and their style, and the tabloids relished every opportunity to compare the two female pop stars. When rumours abounded that Lady Gaga was either a man or a hermaphrodite, Katy's comment about the story (fuelled by clips on YouTube of Gaga performing at Glastonbury in a skimpy outfit with what appeared to be something between her legs) quickly appeared in newspapers worldwide. 'Oh please. It's all very calculated, she knows what she's doing,' Katy told the *Daily Mirror*. 'She put something in her knickers, a mini strap on. Bless her if she does have a dick, but I am certain she doesn't.'

Gaga, meanwhile, claimed in May 2009 that Katy ran over to her in France, eager to be her friend. 'When I was in Marseilles on my way to a show, Katy Perry chased me, shouting, "Lady Gaga, Lady Gaga, I'm a huge fan",' she told *Now* magazine. 'It's funny because I didn't even think Katy knew who I was. I was looking at her and thinking, "You are Katy Perry! How did this happen?" She was so nice.'

Their paths were to cross throughout the year, in the press and in person, as both women were performing at some of the same festivals and awards shows. The question on everybody's lips, however, was this: when Katy Perry and Lady Gaga came up against each other for coveted gongs such as the MTV Video Music Awards and the MTV Europe Awards, which one of them was going to win?

It was spring, 2009, and Katy's star was still on the rise. She had an MTV Award, a platinum-selling album and three hit singles to her name, and was in the midst of a sell-out worldwide tour. Her personal life was going through some changes, too. Rumours started to circulate that Katy was seen out-and-about with her ex-boyfriend Travis McCoy, and that they were back together.

In March, Katy had given an interview to *Cosmopolitan* magazine (for an issue published in May) in which she admitted, 'I don't like being single. I live this fantastic life, full of these magical things, and at the end of the day all I want to do is pick up my phone and share it with someone.

The other day I'd sold a million records in the US and I didn't have anyone to tell. It was actually a really lonely moment.'

She obviously didn't like being single, but did that mean she was back with Travis? Since their break-up at the end of 2008, the press had linked Katy to other men. In February, the press decided she was dating Benji Madden, of the band Good Charlotte, and twin brother of Nicole Richie's husband Joel. The pair were spotted in Las Vegas over the Valentine's Day weekend, where Katy had spent the evening performing at the Hard Rock Hotel's club Wasted Space. From there, she and Benji apparently went to Lavo, a local nightclub, and *People* magazine reported that 'the two conspicuously cuddled throughout the night, later prompting one observer to sense "some chemistry there"'. Apparently Benji 'even danced for Perry during several songs'.

Katy quickly denied the rumours. She wrote on her blog: 'Oh kittens! It's two pseudo famous people sitting next to each other . . . doesn't mean we were bumping uglies! You know I don't just do that with anyone! That's just how the media works, as you can tell. I was there celebrating a really fun show and a boozy valentines with all my good friends. We were like a group of 25! Benji is a nice young fellow, but my heart really belongs to Kitty Purry.'

More romance rumours were to come. In March, singer/songwriter Josh Groban was tipped as the latest man in Katy's life, following an online scoop by Katy's friend Perez Hilton, but Groban denied this through a spokesperson. 'Josh and Katy are very close friends and hang out, but they are not a couple,' the source told *People* magazine.

On 25 April, the *Sun* newspaper in the UK trumpeted

that they had a 'world exclusive' – Katy was back with Travis. McCoy told the *Sun* reporter: 'The break-up sucked. We're back together now – you're the first person I have told that to. I keep thinking about if I had to go through it again and how s***ty it would be.'

'We were moving way too fast,' he added, talking about their break-up in 2008. 'I was being juvenile about the entire thing. Now it's easy breezy. I'm happy and in love.' So was marriage the next step for the reunited couple? 'I'm just enjoying the way things are right now,' he said. 'I'm in no rush to get the ball and chain strapped to my legs.' Very romantic.

It seemed the pair were officially back on in May 2009, as they attended the Life Ball together in Vienna and were spotted kissing after the show. It was another important night in Katy's life, as she had been asked to be the headline act at the prestigious event. The Life Ball is the biggest charity event in Europe that supports people with HIV/AIDS. Founded by the organisation AIDS LIFE, the ball consists of an opening ceremony, with speeches from international stars focusing on raising awareness for AIDS. There are numerous celebrity performances, and almost 4,000 tickets are sold to the public so that they can see the event. Each year the ball has a theme, and some of the tickets are sold as 'Style Tickets' to people who have dressed in the full spirit of the theme and those holding such tickets are allowed to walk the red carpet along with the rich and famous.

There's an opening gala, with performances ranging from opera to pop, and a fashion show as well as dance areas, food areas and bars, all designed to raise money for the cause. It's an impressive event that has become famous outside its home country of Austria, and one that attracts a who's who of celebrities every year.

Sharon Stone, Sir Elton John, Catherine Deneuve, Liza Minnelli, Dita Von Teese and Naomi Campbell are just some of the names who have attended the Life Ball, held at Vienna's city hall and in the square in front of it. It's a truly impressive affair that gets bigger every year. The first ball, in 1993, televised in Austria and Germany, raised less than 100,000 Euros, but at the thirteenth ball in 2005, more than a million Euros were raised, and the event was broadcast throughout Europe with the help of MTV.

It's also a major fashion occasion. Each year, there is a fashion show by a major designer – Thierry Mugler, John Galliano, Vivienne Westwood, Donatella Versace, Missoni and Roberto Cavalli have all held shows featuring famous models such as Alek Wek, Heidi Klum and Naomi Campbell and celebrities including Kylie Minogue, Cyndi Lauper and German actor Udo Kier. And all of them are there to help raise awareness and money for a worthy cause.

Katy wholeheartedly supports the HIV/AIDS cause – the month before, she had designed a T-shirt for high-street fashion store H&M, the proceeds from which also help the fight against AIDS – so was delighted when she was asked to perform at the marine-themed charity gala. She made another spectacular entrance at the event. Dressed in a beautiful white-and-silver gown decorated with starfish and seashells, she was lowered onto the stage in a giant oyster shell. Once on stage, she ripped away the fishtail skirt of her gown to reveal a skimpy corset underneath and performed 'I Kissed a Girl'. She also got to meet some very different icons – *Baywatch* star Pamela Anderson, who appeared in the fashion show, and former US President Bill Clinton, with whom Katy had her picture taken.

And that wasn't all. Especially for the event, Katy had a Mini car designed just for her that would be auctioned afterwards for charity. Each year, the makers of Mini donate a car to be customised for the occasion – the previous year, lingerie designers Agent Provocateur had turned the cute car into a black-and-pink police car, complete with fishnet stocking design on the roof, and pink flashing light on the top. For Katy, creative team The Blonds turned the Mini into an open-top delight, with pink leopard-print paintwork – certainly not a car you could drive without being noticed.

It was a fun night and an extremely successful one, once again raising over a million Euros for AIDS causes. Katy didn't have time to stop and rest after the event, however, as she was due to spend the rest of May back on her world tour, appearing at concerts for her fans in Japan.

She also had time to fit in a concert filmed for *MTV Unplugged*, a show on MTV for artists to showcase their material – usually by performing acoustically, with no electronic instruments. The series began in 1989, with Squeeze among the artists performing their hits in an unplugged fashion. Over the next few years, Paul McCartney, Eric Clapton, Pearl Jam, Duran Duran, Bob Dylan and Nirvana all performed for the series, while a 1995 performance by Kiss signalled the band's re-formation (it had been the first time the original members had performed together since 1979). It was certainly a prestigious programme to be invited on to, with previous attendees Eric Clapton and Tony Bennett both winning Grammys for their *Unplugged* sessions.

Katy recorded her own stripped-down set, featuring rearranged versions of 'Thinking of You', 'Waking Up in Vegas' and 'I Kissed a Girl', as well as a handful of new songs, the never-before-released 'Brick by Brick' and a cover of Fountain of Wayne's 'Hackensack'. As well as the show being broadcast on MTV, the songs were made available for Katy's fans a few months later on CD and DVD, with the DVD also including an interview with Katy filmed on the day of the performance.

'I really wanted to do *MTV Unplugged* obviously because it has such a great history of showing off really who the person is,' she explained. 'I get to do a remix on "I Kissed a Girl" that's a little bit cabaret, a little bit jazz. You get to hear the real story of the songs [when they are performed acoustically], which is important to me.'

Katy also talked about the outfit she chose for the show – a pale pink chiffon evening gown, complemented by flowers in her hair. 'Some people have an idea who I am, a little piece of the cake, but I get to show off really more. I have a larger-than-life personality and my clothes reflect that. For *MTV Unplugged* I wanted to be a mixture of Stevie Nicks and a fairy!'

By June, as she returned to Europe as part of the tour, things were not going so well for Katy, however, and if you believed the newspapers, it appeared she was taking knocks from all sides. First, there were rumours of another split with Travis. On 8 June, he was spotted leaving Las Vegas nightclub Jet with two 'buxom beauties' by his side – neither of which were Katy. McCoy's representative was quick to deny any wrongdoing, saying 'I was not familiar with that story. It sounds really out of character [for Travis].' Katy didn't comment, and the pair insisted that their relationship was still going strong. Indeed, in an interview published at the beginning of June in *Complex* magazine, Katy commented on why she thought Travis was attracted to her in the first place. 'I'm probably going to get in trouble for saying this, but Travis said he was never a boob guy – he was always a butt guy – until he met me,' she laughed. She also scotched any rumours that she was happy to enter into intimacy with strangers, too: 'For me, it's not a pastime, going out and meeting people and trying to hook up with people. That actually makes me feel disgusting. From a really early age, I was really sensitive to that. Getting your flirt on is the best thing in the world, but when it comes to sharing bodily fluids with a person I don't know – no, thank you.'

Being away from Travis on tour was tough, and Katy wasn't faring that well alone in England, where she was staying as part of the ongoing Hello Katy tour. She was preparing to perform in Brighton on 11 June when her tour-bus was broken into. A burglar was arrested by local police before he could steal anything, and Katy wrote on her blog: 'Someone just broke into our bus, they got caught. Luckily all there is is glitter, catsuit outfits, fruit & a box set of *Ab Fab*. Sux fer them.'

It wasn't the only problem she had that week. Following her public spat with Lily Allen, now another female singer had decided to take a pop at Katy in the press. Outspoken singer Beth Ditto, of the band Gossip, launched her own attack in an interview with *Attitude* magazine. 'I hate Katy

Perry. I am so offended. She's just riding on the backs of our culture without having to pay any of the dues and not actually being lesbian or anything at all.' Beth went on to say that Katy was 'offensive to gay culture' and that 'I Kissed a Girl' was 'a boner dyke anthem for straight girls who like to turn guys on by making out or, like, faking gay'.

Raven-haired Ditto was no stranger to controversy, so her comments were perhaps to be expected (although she took her time – 'I Kissed a Girl' had been released over a year before she decided to comment on it). A punk singer from Arkansas ('I think punks usually smell. I don't wear deodorant or bother with shaving my armpits'), she shocked readers when she confessed to the *Sun* that she ate squirrels as a child ('My mum hated us doing it, but all the kids we knew ate squirrels. My cousin just took out his BB gun and started shooting at them out the window, and then he just skinned them and fried them, and ate them just like chicken. We used to play with their tails afterwards . . .'). The larger-than-life gay activist, who is just over five feet tall and weighs fifteen stone, was also criticised by a British doctor for encouraging the growing obesity rates amongst teenagers. Professor Michael McMahon said: 'The increasing profile of larger celebrities, for example Beth Ditto, means that being overweight is now perceived as being normal. We talk about the dangers of skinny media images, but the problem swings both ways. The increased acceptance of obesity is alarming.' It seemed Beth had as many problems with the press as Katy, so it was a shame she decided to attack one of the people who may have understood what it was like to be a female singer in the limelight.

When interviewed by the *London Paper* at *Glamour* magazine's awards lunch a few days after Beth's rant, Katy was asked how she felt about Ditto's nasty comments. 'I don't want to get into a slanging war with anybody so I don't want to say anything bad about her,' she said. 'But I'm not impressed. I've learned in the past year that one artist should never insult another artist's music – it's tacky.'

Ditto didn't take kindly to being called tacky, and in a 19 June interview with *Spinner* magazine, she spoke out again: 'Honestly, I could care less if Katy Perry's impressed with me. I don't care if she writes a song about kissing a girl, but there are people who kiss girls in their everyday life, and it's not as easy as just kissing a girl and everybody loving you. It'd be really rad to hear her talk about something like that.'

Beth went on: 'To Katy, it's just this party song. As a gay person, it's like, "Oh, of course this straight person singing about kissing a girl goes straight to Top Forty and people buy this record. Who can give a f*** about real gay people?" That's what's really painful about the whole thing.' Beth added, 'That's what makes me laugh about "I'm not impressed." It's like, "Oh, that's what you think? Of course, because you never thought about what a real gay person feels, and the impact that a song like that has on the gay world in a time of crucial civil rights."'

Katy wasn't just in Beth Ditto's bad books, either. In June, an Australian fashion designer named Katie Perry went to the press saying she had been threatened with legal action by Katy Perry's lawyers over the use of her name. Katie Perry had started a fashion label in her name two years before, but received a letter asking her to stop trading under that name. 'On 9 June, I went to pick up some mail and received a thirty-page letter from Fisher Adams Kelly, who represent Katheryn Hudson [Katy Perry's real name], opposing the use of my trademark and asking me to pull my trademark, stop using advertising and sign the attached letter or face legal proceedings,' said the Sydney-based designer to SmartCompany.com. 'I started my label before she was known here. I've worked hard building up my brand, everything is made in Australia, I'm building up a great reputation, and to have someone receive those statements from lawyers saying I can't do that is distressing. It's also intimidating; I've never had to deal with lawyers and legal things like this before.'

Katy (the singer) was quick to clear things up and state that she wasn't actually suing Katie (the designer) at all. On 20 June, Katy posted a message on her blog to clarify matters. She wrote: 'In the course of securing trademark protection for "Katy Perry" in Australia, it came to the attention of her representatives that Katie Howell, a clothing designer in Australia, had filed an application for trademark protection under a similar name in connection with her own clothing design business. A routine notice letter was sent to Ms Howell, as is customary in trademark practice, alerting her of Ms Perry's intended application. This is a routine trademark application, and I certainly haven't sued anyone. As usual, some of the press seems to have delighted in creating a story where there is none.'

Despite it all sounding like the matter had been resolved, Katie Perry the designer – perhaps seeing an opportunity to get some press attention – then took to YouTube to send a message to her almost namesake. Filmed with the Sydney Opera House behind her, Katie says in the video: 'This is a message to Katy Perry the singer. This is the only way I know to contact you so I hope you hear this. I am an Aussie girl doing my dream of making Australian made loungewear . . . I am absolutely no threat whatsoever to you and I welcome you to come and visit my studio when you come and give a concert here in August but at the moment the only people who are making any money from this are the lawyers.'

'I would love for you to get in contact with me . . . I'd love to speak to you and hopefully between the two of us we can sort something out . . . I wish you all the success but leave me to carry on my dream.'

Perhaps Katy listened, because on 18 July, Katie stated on her own blog, in a post entitled 'It's All Over', that any legal activity over the trademark would not be ongoing: 'It started with a legal letter and ended with a fax. The battle against my trademark is finished with the withdrawal of opposition from the singer, Katy Perry's lawyers. It is amazing to think that it is all over.' Katie went so far as to organise a celebration following the announcement, on 20 August. 'I wanted to show thanks to my supporters and celebrate the end of the trademark battle,' she wrote on the blog, describing an evening of wine and celebration at her design studio.

Katy's team was perhaps a little sensitive about the bad press she had received over such a small thing. When Katy appeared on TV in Australia in August, her manager jumped the gun a little when Katy was asked a certain question. According to the *Sun* newspaper, reporter Nuala Hafner started to ask Katy 'Who's your favourite Australian . . . ' and before she could answer, her manager – worried, perhaps that the end of the question was 'designer' – cut the power to the studio lights and the interview was plunged into darkness. The interview quickly resumed with Katy apologising, and Hafner later told reporters: 'She was just delightful and keen to make amends. She calmed him [her manager] down, and after several apologies, the interview resumed.'

Katy must have wondered what on earth would happen to her next. And yes, there was more controversy around the corner.

Before Katy had released and recorded *One of the Boys*, she had posed for a variety of promotional photos taken by fashion photographer Terry Richardson, some of which were intended for her website or for the album cover. One of them, in which Katy has a shaggy Joan Jett-style haircut and is wearing a torn T-shirt, shows her holding a knife up to her cheek with its tip pointing at her eye. The photo was clearly old, but when the pictures resurfaced in the *Sun* newspaper once Katy became a star, the press had a field day. A source at Katy's record company told the *Sun*: 'The knife picture was done to give Katy more of a sexy, harder edge. But in the end it wasn't picked as a main shot for her album or website.'

Unfortunately, campaigners against knife violence in the UK – where, in 2008 there had been sixty teenage deaths due to street violence – took offence at the photo. Richard Taylor, the father of murder victim Damilola Taylor, the schoolboy fatally stabbed on a Peckham housing estate in 2000, told the press: 'This woman's behaviour is unacceptable. She must be out of her mind to pose for a picture like this. There is nothing glamorous about knives, they wreck families. Any youngsters seeing her will think it is OK to carry a blade.'

Katy's response was to post another picture on her website – one of her holding a spoon in the same way she had held the knife in the original picture. Underneath it said: 'I do condone eating ice cream with a very large spoon.' While Katy was obviously trying to make light of a situation that had gone out of control – after all, it was an old photo, and not one that had been intended for use – her response further incensed Mr Taylor. 'She's lost all of her integrity by this. It would have been better for her to have apologised. Youngsters would have seen that and taken it as something positive. Instead, she has decided to challenge us,' he told the *Sun*.

Katy's publicist then stepped in, releasing a statement on Katy's behalf. 'Katy Perry is against all violence. The photo in question was taken in 2005 and is in no way related to the current events in the UK.' In an interview with Lewis Bazley, Katy responded to the *Sun*'s printing of the old photo that started the whole furore in the first place. 'It's a tabloid. That's what their job is. It's an unfortunate situation and really it was just a misrepresentation of a coincidence that had no correlation to what's going on here,' she said, referring to the *Sun*'s tactic of printing the picture at the same time that knife crime was in the headlines in the UK every day. 'I did a long photoshoot with lots of props in my hands and they just chose that one. It wasn't anything I was ever hiding, it was on my MySpace page. I think if people really want to believe that stuff [about me, they will], but I think anybody that uses both sides of their brain will understand to take some of that stuff [in the press] with a grain of salt.'

It seemed no matter what Katy did, or didn't do, she sparked press interest and the paparazzi were now just as interested in her personal life as in her music. She made a jokey comment about swine flu, and within hours it had made the papers. 'Since swine flu is super trendy I wanted to make sure I was in style with my swine flu ring!' she wrote. 'I got this one in Miami at Big Drop the other day . . . a flying piggy. Kitty Purry was telling me the other night that she remembers when bird flu was in and now pig flu is cool and she wonders when kitty flu is gonna hit, as she would like to be more popular than she currently already is . . . fame whore.' Katy was obviously not intending to make light of swine flu, but her comments – and the photo of the sparkly pink pig ring – appeared worldwide.

Then, on 6 September, Katy was spotted wearing a different ring that sent the paparazzi into a frenzy – a diamond ring on her wedding finger during a night out in Los Angeles. Could she and Travis be engaged?

Neither side was talking. There had been rumours of an engagement between them once before, in December 2008, just before they broke up, so no one knew for sure. However, just seven days after being spotted wearing that ring, Katy was seen doing something else that made people wonder whether she was still with Travis at all.

It was 13 September 2009, and time for the MTV Video Music Awards in New York. The nominations had been announced the month before, and Katy was possibly in line for Best Female Video (for 'Hot n Cold'). Her pop rival Lady Gaga was nominated for nine, as was Beyoncé, while Britney Spears was up for seven awards.

The awards were to be held at the iconic Radio City Music Hall in New York. Known as the Showplace of the Nation, it is part of the Rockefeller Center on Sixth Avenue, and was first opened in 1932. For most of its first few decades, the Art Deco-style Radio City Music Hall was the place to see new movies, complete with a lavish stage show, but after a refurbishment in 1980 it became home to concerts and live stage shows, including the famous Christmas Spectacular that takes place every year and features the dance team known as the Rockettes. Artists such as Frank Sinatra, Liberace, Stevie Wonder, Celine Dion and Ella Fitzgerald all performed at Radio City Music Hall, and it has also played host to the Grammys and the theatre awards The Tonys. It was a perfect venue for MTV to hold its own awards bash.

It was an interesting night. Held three months after the death of Michael Jackson, the awards were dedicated to him. Madonna opened the show with a speech about the King of Pop, and then Michael's sister Janet Jackson appeared to introduce a musical tribute to him and his career. Then the show proper began. And there was Katy, with Aerosmith guitarist Joe Perry, singing Queen's 'We Will Rock You' to open the event. In a white corset studded with red rhinestones and shiny trousers, she rocked the house and her song heralded the entrance of that evening's host, Russell Brand.

While Russell had made some outrageous comments (in the view of the press, at least) as host at the previous year's VMAs (he had called President George Bush 'a retarded cowboy fella', for a start), his performance in 2009 was not what made the front of the newspapers the following day. It wasn't Katy's or Lady Gaga's risqué outfits that produced column inches, either. Instead it was something that happened during young singer Taylor Swift's speech when she went up to accept the award for Best Female Video for her song 'You Belong to Me'. It was a surprise win, as many people had expected Beyoncé's iconic 'Single Ladies' to secure the prize. And while Taylor was accepting the award, rapper/singer Kanye West thought it was a good idea to jump up onto the stage and interrupt her. 'Yo, Tay, I'm really happy for you and I'mma let you finish, but Beyoncé had one of the best videos of all time!' The camera cut to Beyoncé, who looked understandably shocked (as did poor Taylor), and the audience began to boo at Kanye, who was then removed from the show.

Later in the evening, Beyoncé won Video of the Year for 'Single Ladies', and she graciously asked Taylor to join her on stage so she could finish her acceptance speech. It was an event that would rage on for weeks in the press. Stars took to their blogs and Twitter to denounce Kanye West's behaviour, with Pink tweeting 'Kanye West is the biggest piece of **** on earth. Quote me.' Kelly Clarkson blogged: 'What happened to you as a child? Did you not get hugged enough?' and Katy let her feelings be known about it, too, saying 'F*** you, Kanye. It's like you stepped on a kitten.'

West did post an apology on his own blog, and also apologised on the *Jay Leno Show*, while Taylor talked about what happened on *The View*. 'I think my overall thought process was like, "Wow, I can't believe I won, this is awesome, don't trip and fall, I'm gonna get to thank the fans, this is so cool. Oh, Kanye West is here. Cool haircut. What are you doing there?" And then, "Ouch". And then, "I guess I'm not gonna get to thank the fans.'" West later made a personal apology to Taylor, which she accepted.

Behind the scenes, something else was going on. Lothario Russell Brand admitted on stage that he had his eye on Katy Perry ('Katy Perry didn't win an award and she's staying at the same hotel as me, so she's gonna need a shoulder to cry on. So in a way, I'm the real winner tonight'), whom he had discovered was staying in the suite next to his at the Soho Grand Hotel in Manhattan. According to his autobiography *Booky Wook 2*, Russell's friend and manager, Nik Linnen, had warned him to stay away from her with the words: 'Be careful, mate. They've got her down to do your intro [at the awards], the last thing we need is you ballsin' it up by givin' her one the night before the show . . . What if you upset her? You'll have it off with her and then she'll see you doing the maid or some groupie or your assistant or make-up person or the bell boy!'

Russell says he told Nik: 'You have my word as an Englishman, I shall not seduce Miss Perry till *after* the show.' Without knowing Russell's plans, Katy made her own presence known to him backstage in an unusual fashion. 'I was drinking a bottle of water, I'd finished it, it was empty and I saw him across the room,' she told interviewer Rebecca Twomey. 'I literally just thought, hmm, that man, big hair, empty bottle of water, and I threw it in this subliminal modern-day cupid sort of way and it hit him right on the head.'

In *Booky Wook 2*, Russell remembers the event, too, though slightly differently. 'The bottle hit me right on the head and although it was plastic, it was half full or half empty, depending on your perspective, and it hurt. Everyone laughed. What had I done to deserve such insubordination? I surveyed the missile's trajectory for clues to reveal the culprit, and there she stood.'

Russell continues, remembering Katy's first comment after throwing the bottle: '"Got you on the head there, huh? Kind of an easy target, it's so big and you've got that ridiculous hair . . ."' The pair traded insults, but when Russell complimented Katy on her bracelet (an Alexander McQueen bangle with twin skulls), she placed it on his wrist. 'Throughout [the show] I carried the bracelet in my pocket,' Russell wrote, 'even though she was there.' Brand was obviously smitten, and the pair were spotted that evening at Lady Gaga's aftershow party at New York club Avenue.

An insider told US gossip column Page Six: 'They were sitting very close together, flirting and whispering to each other with their faces very close. Then Russell leaned in for a long kiss. It didn't look like this was the first time. He was looking extremely pleased with himself.'

MTV.com noted that Katy was supposedly still with Travis McCoy, and decided, bearing in mind Russell's history, that they would give the romance 'two weeks – tops'. No one expected the British comedian with a reputation for bedding hundreds of women and the young American pop star from a religious background to hit it off. No one expected the flirtation to last. And no one expected what happened next . . .

7

Russell Brand

Grays in Essex is a long way from the sun-drenched beaches of Santa Barbara, where Katy grew up. But it was there, at midnight on 4 June 1975, that Barbara and Ron Brand welcomed little Russell Edward into the world, the boy who would one day grow up to win the hand of a beautiful American pop star.

His background couldn't have been more different from his bride-to-be's. Grays is a large town in the Thurrock area of Essex, about 20 miles east of London, and is best known for the large nearby indoor shopping centre of Lakeside. Before Russell, perhaps the best-known people to have come from Grays were *Threads* director Mick Jackson, actor Phil Davis and squeaky-voiced comedian Joe Pasquale.

His childhood differed greatly from Katy's, too. Within six months of Russell's birth, his parents had separated. From then on, as Russell describes in his first autobiography, *My Booky Wook*, his father was 'a sporadic presence, affording me cyclonic visits at the weekend. He would invariably arrive late, to find me ready and waiting for him, all dressed up and mummified in my duffel coat . . . then a huge argument would ensue, which would generally end with both my mother and myself in tears.'

Without his father around, Russell was surrounded by women: his mum, his dad's sisters Janet and Joan, plus family friends Auntie Brenda, Auntie Pat and Auntie Josie. They were there as support when his mother was diagnosed with cancer and had a hysterectomy when he was seven years old, and then again four years later when she was treated for breast cancer.

Russell wasn't the easiest of children, getting into trouble in and out of school on a regular basis, so by the time he was a teenager he was sent to boarding school, where, instead of studying, he learnt that he had the ability to make people laugh. 'As we all lay in bed at night, I would conjure up pornographic stories from the depths of my own dirty brainbox and prattle them out to my disciples,' he remembers in his autobiography. He was later expelled after a girl was found under his bed in his dorm (they hadn't been up to anything but had hidden when a prefect came into the room), and then sent to the local comprehensive in Grays. It was there that the seeds of a future lothario were sown.

In his book, Russell writes about a troubled time as a teenager, when he cut himself and became bulimic after he was bullied at school for being fat ('It was really unusual in boys, quite embarrassing. But I found it euphoric,' he told the *Observer*). This was also the time when he first discovered he had a talent for acting and performing, appearing as Fat Sam in a school production of *Bugsy Malone*, and then winning a place at the Italia Conti stage school when he was sixteen. While Italia Conti gave him the opportunity to act (and meet girls), it was at the school that Russell was first introduced to drugs, a habit that would plague him in the years before he knew Katy. 'I started at sixteen smoking stuff and drinking a lot,' he told the *Daily Mail*. 'I was bulimic when I was fourteen. I had problems with food and self-harming, I've always had these odd compulsive traits looking for an outlet. I started with loads of grass and hash, then took loads of amphetamines, then loads of acid, then loads of Ecstasy and loads of coke, till in the end I took loads of crack and heroin.'

By the end of his first year at Italia Conti, the school opted not to continue Russell's tuition, due to his drug-taking, so by 1992 – around the time that a young Katy was making her singing debut in Santa Barbara – he had left home, was looking for work and was also continually getting into trouble. Despite being arrested in connection with marijuana and then continuing to take drugs, however, he managed to secure a place at an acting academy in London called the Drama Centre, only to be thrown out after a year, following one too many incidents. It wasn't all bad, however – within weeks he was working on comedy sketches with one of his Drama Centre friends, and was on his way to becoming a working comedian.

In 2000, on the other side of the Atlantic, Katy was recording her first album as Katy Hudson, a CD that would never have a proper release. In England, a still drug-addled Russell Brand was carving out a career as a stand-up comic, first with pal Karl Theobald, in an act entitled Theobald & Brand on Ice, then as a solo act in small clubs around London. This led to him being invited to the final of Hackney Empire's New Act of the Year competition – the first round had been in a pub in front of a small crowd, but the final was played out before an audience of two thousand. Russell came fourth in the competition, so didn't walk away with a prize, but he did meet his first agent, Nigel Klarfeld, and the two comedians with whom he would make his Edinburgh Festival debut, Mark Felgate and Shappi Khorsandi.

His career was on the rise. Aged just twenty-five, Russell was contacted by some MTV producers who had seen him perform in Edinburgh, and who asked if he would like to audition in London to be the host of one of their shows, *Dancefloor Chart*. It was a perfect job for him – all Russell had to do was go to clubs in the UK and abroad (including some on the island of Ibiza in the summer) and interview the clubbers, many of whom were as stoned as he was. Unfortunately, Russell's womanising and drug-taking got him into trouble with MTV, too – in *My Booky Wook* he recounts charging lap dances and prostitutes to the MTV publicist's credit card, having a lap dancer delivered to his flat using the TV station's cab account, and using the same car company to run his errands – whether it was driving his mum around or picking up drugs.

It was what he did on 12 September 2001, however, that was the final straw with MTV. As well as deciding to bring his drug-dealer Gritty and Gritty's daughter to work, and introducing them both to Kylie Minogue, Russell turned up that day at the MTV studios – the day after the planes had struck the twin towers of the World Trade Center in New York, killing thousands – dressed in a white tunic, fake beard and a tea towel on his head. He was effectively dressed as Osama bin Laden, and – needless to say – MTV fired him.

If Katy had met Russell at this period in his life, drugged-up and destructive, she would no doubt have run a mile. But while she was working on songs with Glen Ballard in sunny Los Angeles, aged just seventeen, twenty-six-year-old Russell was making a name for himself in London as an erratic, occasionally genius-like, troublemaker who seemingly couldn't hold down a job. After losing his position at MTV, he made a documentary/comedy series *RE:Brand* for a cable channel called UK Play, and also secured his own radio slot on Xfm as a presenter. Since the MTV Osama stunt, he had become a famous name in the tabloids, and they were all waiting to see what controversial thing Russell Brand would do next.

They didn't have to wait very long. Russell first irked the producers of his Xfm show by bringing in a homeless friend named James to appear on the Sunday lunchtime programme. Russell introduced him as 'Homeless James, your homeless agony uncle – for all your homeless needs', and when no callers phoned in with problems, Russell proceeded to read out the pornographic problems that feature on the agony page of the tabloid newspaper the *Sunday Sport*. The next day he was fired.

He was also fired from an acting role in the comedy *Cruise of the Gods*, where he was to appear alongside David Walliams, Rob Brydon and Steve Coogan, following some ill-advised drug use and visits to brothels while filming on location in the Greek islands and Istanbul (his role in the one-off

TV show is fleeting), so when he signed to a new management agency, the first thing they did was encourage him to
go into recovery to kick his habit.

By December 2002, Russell was in treatment, and in
the spring of 2003 he had completed his recovery course
and moved into a flat in Hampstead, North London, with
his cat Morrissey. His agent, John Noel, encouraged him to
try out for more TV work, and Russell went to the audition
that would completely transform his career. John also represented Davina McCall, who had become a household name
thanks to her presenting job on *Big Brother*. When John
learned that Channel 4 wanted to make a debate show to
accompany the fifth series of the reality show, he sent along
Russell to audition for it. 'I just had to say what I thought
[about some footage from a previous *Big Brother* episode]
and muck about with researchers pretending to be guests
or audience members. That went really well . . . but before
they would finally offer it to me, John had to sign a personal
contract guaranteeing that I'd be no trouble.'

Originally titled *Big Brother's Efourum* (it was first shown
on cable channel E4) when it was broadcast in 2004, the show
was later retitled *Big Brother's Big Mouth* and transferred to
Channel 4, where it won even larger audiences. Russell was a
star, and he was clean from drugs at last, but there was more
controversy to come.

During 2006, while Katy was struggling to land a record
deal in LA, Russell was riding high on his fame in the UK.
After spending time in a US clinic for sex addiction, he
returned to the stage for a series of confessional stand-
up performances in which he talked about his addictions,

embarrassing moments in his career, and his relationship with the tabloid press. While he talked about the events of his past on stage, his present sounded just as chaotic.

In the summer of 2006, he was asked to present the *NME* Awards, a ceremony in which gongs are given out to rock luminaries by the British weekly music magazine. Throughout the event, Russell made jokes about some of the assembled stars, but one amongst them didn't find it funny. When Sir Bob Geldof went up to accept his award for Best DVD for *Live 8*, he began his speech by saying: 'Russell Brand, what a c***.' Russell responded: 'It's no wonder Bob Geldof knows so much about famine – he's been dining out on "I Don't Like Mondays" for thirty years.' In an interview with the *Observer* a few weeks later, Russell confessed to interviewer Barbara Ellen that he had been quite surprised by Geldof's outburst. 'This is a saint – a man who's been canonised, and to use such antiquated Anglo-Saxon language in such an aggressive way. I really was surprised. It's Bob Geldof! And he's achieved things beyond . . . well, instead of, music, which is really admirable. I've been told since by numerous people whose opinion I respect, Noel Gallagher for instance, and Carl Barât [of Dirty Pretty Things] that he misjudged the room, and it was just embarrassing and awkward. There was a part of me that needed that confirmation.'

It didn't stop Russell from being asked to present other awards shows, including the 2007 Brit Awards, part of *Comic Relief*, and the UK section of Live Earth at Wembley in July 2007. He even appeared on stage in front of the Queen and the Duke of Edinburgh at the 2007 *Royal Variety Performance*, treading the boards of the Liverpool Empire Theatre alongside comedian Al Murray, rock band Bon Jovi, the English National Ballet and comedy stalwart Jimmy Tarbuck.

It was also in 2007 that he resigned from *Big Brother's Big Mouth*. In a statement to BBC News, he thanked Channel 4 for 'taking the risk of employing an ex-junkie twerp' and said: 'The three years I've spent on *Big Brother's Big Mouth* have been an unprecedented joy. *Big Mouth* has afforded me opportunities that are too exciting to turn down, so alas I can do it no more. And whilst I recognize this isn't as significant as the resignation of Beckham or the Cuban missile crisis, I just wanted to say thanks to everyone.'

The opportunities of which he spoke included the offer of an acting role in a movie and a return to radio, although if you believed the tabloids, Russell would have a hard time fitting in such work between all his extra-curricular activities. The *Sun* newspaper had branded him their Shagger of the Year in November 2006, and again the following year, in recognition of the series of girlfriends he had been seen out and about with (in his honour, the award was later renamed by the *Sun* as the Russell Brand Shagger of the Year Award). In his second autobiography, *Booky Wook 2: This Time It's Personal*, he admitted his conquests pre-Katy had included supermodel Kate Moss, who had asked to meet him after seeing him on Jonathan Ross's chat-show, Makosi, one of the *Big Brother* contestants, and Becki Seddiki, another former housemate who sold her story to the tabloids.

When it was revealed that Russell was dating Kate Moss, Becki sent her a warning via the newspapers: 'I wish Kate would find a man to settle down with, but that's not Russell. All he's interested in is sh****g, and it's all about his enjoyment, never the woman's. I hope Kate is prepared to pleasure him in bed and not to expect anything in return – because that's what Russell is like. Kate might like her men dirty, but she's going to get bored with him pretty soon. They might both be enjoying some dirty sex, but it won't last. It isn't a relationship, with Russell – it's about sex. I spent a lot of time satisfying him and used all my best techniques. But he didn't reciprocate. After he'd got his pleasure, he just rolled over and went to sleep.'

Hers was not the only kiss-and-tell-style story about Russell to make the papers. The *Sunday Mirror* newspaper went so far as to send an undercover female reporter to rout out his sexual secrets. The reporter accompanied Russell back to his flat after a night out. Two days later an exclusive article appeared in the *Sunday Mirror*.

The article was packed with quotes from the journalist and titled 'Night I Was Branded'. The reporter, Nikhita Mahajan, reported that Russell said: 'I am a sexy Wildman, you're nice and soft. Let me touch you and stuff.'

Russell found an opportunity to respond on his new radio show for BBC 6. 'Entrapment is what it is,' he said. 'She was this journalist coming back to my flat offering, err, fun to say the least, but she turned out to be tiresome. Turns out it was all a big trick to write about me. She should be ashamed. She has told needless, senseless lies about old Russ. Remember I'm single, with no kids. So if after a gig a girl swans up to me, I think "nice". It's a bit of a hobby.'

He described the story as 'a kiss-and-tell tale without any kiss' and said that the words he supposedly spoke to her were 'odd and untrue'. 'I don't say stuff like that,' he added. 'I never said any of them things. I'd be so embarrassed to say that.'

Such reports further cemented his lothario, ladies' man image, however, and infuriated newspapers such as the *Daily Mail*, who printed the following when Russell's BBC6 Music programme, *The Russell Brand Show*, was due to be transferred to the more traditional station Radio 2: 'Drug addict. Sex addict. Bin Laden impersonator. Is Russell Brand REALLY what Radio 2 needs?' wrote *Mail* journalist Alison Boshoff, leading Russell to leave a message on the *Mail*'s answering machine (a tactic that would later get him into a lot of trouble) that said: 'What, the *Daily Mail* not answering their phone, what are they doing, driving immigrants out of the country with a sharpened stick?' he said, live on air.

The press couldn't decide whether they loved or hated Russell Brand, but the public loved him. The radio show was a success on Radio 2, and Russell had also been given a role in the new *St. Trinian's* movie, as the character Flash Harry (the spiv played by George Cole in the original films). As most Brits over a certain age know, St. Trinian's is a school filled with naughty girls. Based on cartoons by Ronald Searle, the original five films were made between 1954 and 1980 and featured classic British comedy actors including Alastair Sim, Joyce Grenfell and Sid James.

The 2007 remake featured such stars as Rupert Everett (playing two characters, including – in drag – the role of Miss Fritton, head of the school), Colin Firth, Stephen Fry and, as some of the cheeky schoolgirls up to no good, model Lily Cole, Gemma Arterton and Talulah Riley. The reviews weren't great, alas. 'Russell Brand, unable to do his own material, is uncomfortable in the laugh-free role of Flash Harry,' said Peter Bradshaw in the *Guardian*, while the BBC review stated that 'Brand was treated as an afterthought'.

Happily, for Russell, the reviews didn't matter as he already had another movie lined up. After filming *St. Trinian's*, he had flown to Los Angeles for meetings about an additional acting role, this time in a movie produced by Judd Apatow, the director of hit comedies *The 40-Year-Old Virgin* and *Knocked Up* and the producer of successful films including *Superbad* and *Anchorman*.

Russell had auditioned for the role of Aldous Snow, but he also had to try a screen test with Kristen Bell, who was to play the part of Sarah Marshall herself. 'Kristen Bell is obviously a razzle-dazzle, titchy likkle wonk-eyed pebble of wonder, and the reading with her was a laugh,' he added. 'Everyone said we had chemistry and my casting was once and for all approved – I was to be the supporting lead in a big, Hollywood romantic comedy.'

Filming involved a three-month shoot at the Turtle Bay Resort in Oahu, Hawaii. The location had already been used in episodes of *Hawaii 5-0* and *Magnum, P.I.*, and it offers stunning views as well as two golf courses, ten tennis courts, pools and a spa. This was to be Russell's home for the spring of 2007, alongside his co-stars, who also included Jonah Hill, Jason Segel (who wrote the movie), Paul Rudd and Mila Kunis. Of course, Russell admits in *Booky Wook 2* that he couldn't help but hit on his co-stars, first Kristen (who had a boyfriend) and then Mila. 'Mila casually revealed she too had a boyfriend. Then . . . she added that her sweetheart was the little boy out of *Home Alone* [Macaulay Culkin]. Initially I was disgusted, thinking her some kind of sexy, female nonce, then I remembered that fifteen years had passed since then and he would probably be an adult by now.'

The plot of the movie was simple, and funny. After Peter (Segel) is dumped by his girlfriend Sarah Marshall (Bell), he takes a trip to Hawaii, only to discover that Sarah is there with her new boyfriend, British rock star Aldous Snow (Russell, who even sings a song as Aldous on the soundtrack). While Peter begins a friendship with hotel receptionist Rachel (Kunis), Sarah becomes jealous, resulting in a scene where she tries to have loud sex with Aldous to make Peter, in an adjacent room with Rachel, jealous.

The movie was a hit when it was released in the spring of 2008. 'Brand's a rather brilliant comedian and no small asset to the picture,' said the *Village Voice*, while the *San Francisco Chronicle* commented: 'The major surprise is Russell Brand as Aldous, the rock star. Instead of a comic abstraction, Aldous is presented with some complexity and sympathy, and he's played to comic perfection by Brand, who's a welcome discovery.'

Forgetting Sarah Marshall was, for Russell Brand, much more than just a successful movie. Just after the film was released, Katy Perry was enjoying her own success with her first major hit single, 'I Kissed a Girl', and – thanks to his role as Aldous Snow – it wouldn't be long before the two future spouses would first cross paths.

When he wasn't making movies, during 2008 Russell continued to film TV shows for the BBC (*Russell Brand on the Road*) and Channel 4 (*Ponderland*) as well as present his Saturday evening programme on Radio 2. He was also asked to host one of the biggest awards shows held in the USA – the MTV Video Music Awards. The choice of Russell as presenter was an unusual one – he was not yet especially well known in the USA, despite the success of *Forgetting Sarah Marshall*, and he also had a reputation for saying things at these occasions that would shock – something MTV may not have wanted for a show that is broadcast around the world. He didn't disappoint. During his opening monologue at the awards on 7 September 2008, Russell talked about the upcoming US presidential elections and his support for Barack Obama. 'Some people, I think they're called racists, say America is not ready for a black president,' he said. 'But I know America to be a forward-thinking country because otherwise why would you have let that retarded cowboy fella be president for eight years? We were very impressed. We thought it was nice of you to let him have a go, because, in England, he wouldn't be trusted with a pair of scissors.'

The controversy continued when he made fun of the Jonas Brothers' promise rings (he later apologised), and said Britney Spears was 'a female Christ'. In fact, some viewers were so incensed that Russell began to receive death threats after the awards. 'The VMAs were a lot of fun. Especially the death threats. If you are going to kill someone, don't give them advance notice, which gives you a chance to prepare,' he said to BBC Radio 1: 'These Christian Republicans were watching me and thought, "Well, this is no good, I shall do a death threat." How can you, while watching the TV, think, "Oh I don't enjoy this, no I'm not enjoying this at all," then think, "Right, I'm going to kill him"? That's a huge jump.'

While the awards marked another headline-grabbing point in Russell's career, they will also be remembered for his first meeting with Katy Perry. Just before the awards were taking place, Russell had heard that his character, Aldous Snow (from *Forgetting Sarah Marshall*) would be getting his own spin-off movie, which would also star Jonah Hill. As Aldous is a rock star, the film-makers thought it would be a good idea to feature some real-life rock and pop stars in cameo roles in the movie, which was to be titled *Get Him to the Greek*. And the perfect place to film these cameos would be backstage at the Video Music Awards. Pink and Christina Aguilera filmed scenes with Russell in character as Aldous, and then Katy Perry was asked if she would also appear in the movie. Russell describes his first meeting with her in his book: 'There she stood, Katy Perry, on a fictional street surrounded by people grooming and protecting her, as I sliced the air around her like Serengeti grass. A good-looking young woman, I observed, with mischief in her eyes that met mine, unblinking.' The scene involved the pair sharing a kiss. 'We kissed,' he writes. 'And there was nothing unreal about it. This was not a fictional kiss, our mouths met and there on the Hollywood set I was lost with her in a swirl . . . and this vast, immaculate world created for telling tales had witnessed the start to my favourite story.'

The UK press had reported the controversies of the MTV Video Music Awards with tongue firmly in cheek, amused that Americans are so easily offended when one of their presidents is insulted on national television. Just weeks later, however, Russell was to do something that would almost ruin his career – along with that of another presenter.

It was all about a phone call. On Thursday, 16 October, Russell recorded his radio show with frequent guest Jonathan Ross, to be broadcast two days later. During the show, Ross joked about an interview they had planned with actor Andrew Sachs, best known as Manuel in the 1970s sit-com *Fawlty Towers*. Ross joked that he expected Russell to say he 'had a go on his daughter' as that was the sort of thing he would expect his friend to say.

Russell replied that he actually knew Sachs' granddaugh-ter, Georgina Baillie, that she had visited his home, and was a member of a 'baroque dance group called satanicsluts.com'. He continued: 'She always said to me, "Don't mention that to my granddad Manuel", and now here we are. So when we talk to Manuel, don't mention that his granddaughter's a satanic slut.'

For some reason, the interview with Sachs didn't go ahead so Ross and Brand decided to phone Sachs to ask him why. They got his answer-machine instead, and left several messages.

In the first, Jonathan Ross blurts out: 'He f***ed your granddaughter ... I'm sorry, I apologise. Andrew, I apologise, I got excited, what can I say? It just came out.'

Russell then speaks: 'Andrew Sachs, I did not do nothing with Georgina – oh no, I've revealed I know her name. Oh no, it's a disaster.' Ross goes on to say: 'If he's like most people of a certain age, he's probably got a picture of his grandchildren when they're young right by the phone. So while he's listen-ing to the messages, he's looking at a picture of her, about nine, on a swing ... '

The second message has Russell apologising. 'Andrew, this is Russell Brand. I'm so sorry about the last message, it was part of the radio show – it was a mistake.' Ross then adds: 'It might be true but we didn't want to break it to you in such a harsh way.' Russell adds: 'No, I'm sorry, I'll do any-thing. I wore a condom. Put the phone down. Oh, what's going to happen?'

The third message made things even worse. Ross said: 'She was bent over the couch . . . ', and Russell then impro-vises a song which includes the lines: 'I said some things I didn't of oughta, like I had sex with your granddaughter . . . '

And the fourth and final message didn't make it better, either. 'Alright, Andrew Sachs' answer-phone? I'm ever so so sorry for what I said about Andrew Sachs,' says Russell.

'Just say sorry,' says Ross.

'I'll kill you,' says Russell, laughing.

'Don't say you'll wear him as a hat – just say sorry,' adds Ross.

'Sorry, right,' finishes Russell.

Uh-oh. What exactly happened next has been debated in the press and the full sequence of events is unclear but what seems to have happened is that the show's producer believed that permission for the calls to be broadcast, slightly toned down, had been requested from Andrew Sachs and that this had been granted. However, Sachs denied this and the sub-sequent OFCOM regulator's report found that the necessary informed consent had not been obtained.

The tapes were aired, uncut, on Russell's show on Saturday, 18 October, and the BBC received two complaints the next day – one specifically about the Andrew Sachs mes-sages. A journalist from the *Mail on Sunday* then contacted Andrew Sachs' agent, Meg Pool, asking for comment, and the broadcast was played to him. Sachs was then quoted as saying that it left him 'offended very much indeed'.

The *Daily Mail* began regular attacks on Russell and Jonathan Ross. Russell explained it like this in his book: 'The *Daily Mail* doesn't like me or Jonathan. Jonathan is the most highly paid broadcaster in the country yet came from a working-class background; his demeanour and attitude could be described as anti-establishment, he is cheeky, smart and fearless. In the eyes of the *Daily Mail* I am a heroin addict fornicator with no respect for the system. The *Daily Mail* want junkies dead, not cavorting around on the telly making money and living it up with thousands of beautiful women.'

On 26 October, the *Mail on Sunday* reported that the BBC could face prosecution over the calls, while the BBC announced that it 'was not aware of receiving a complaint from Mr Sachs'. Suddenly, a foolish conversation broadcast to a smallish Radio 2 audience had become national news. Tabloids scrabbled to write about it and to track down Andrew Sachs' granddaughter, and – nine days after it was broadcast – the BBC recorded more than 1,500 complaints about the show (presumably from people who had read about it in the papers, but who had not actually heard it themselves). The BBC issued an apology, stating 'We have received a letter of complaint from Mr Sachs' agent and would like to sincerely apologise to Mr Sachs for the offence caused. We recognise that some of the content broadcast was unacceptable and offensive. We are reviewing how this came about and are responding to Mr Sachs personally. We also apologise to listeners for any offence caused.'

Both Russell and Jonathan then issued private apologies to Sachs, as the number of complaints climbed to over

4,000. By Tuesday, 28 October, the media regulator OFCOM announced an official enquiry into BBC practices, the BBC launched an investigation into how the tapes were passed for broadcast, and politicians including David Cameron and then-culture secretary Andy Burnham asked for an investigation while then-Prime Minister Gordon Brown called the affair 'clearly inappropriate and unacceptable'.

The following day, an interview with Georgina Baillie appeared in the *Sun*, where she described Russell and Jonathan as 'beyond contempt'. Both of the presenters were suspended by the BBC – news that Baillie told the *Sun* she was thrilled to hear: 'Me and my granddad are both really happy'. By the end of 29 October, Russell had announced he was quitting the BBC Radio 2 show altogether.

'It's so typical of the English in general – 10,000 people get outraged, but only five days after it has happened,' Noel Gallagher, a friend of both Jonathan and Russell, told the press in their defence. 'You know what? There's now a massive divide. Them and us.'

The story played out for days and days. Jonathan was suspended from the BBC for twelve weeks without pay, while the Radio 2 controller handed in her resignation. The BBC was later fined £150,000 and OFCOM announced that the tapes 'should never have been broadcast'.

Since then, Russell has revealed that the Andrew Sachs messages were an error in judgement on his part, admitting that it must have been upsetting for Andrew.

The press even reported that Russell was fleeing the country in shame, whereas, in fact, he had to leave behind the debacle in order to begin filming scenes for *Get Him to the Greek*. It seemed that the story – dubbed 'Sachsgate' in the press – didn't look like it was going to go away.

Of course, stories *do* go away, especially when the subject of the tabloids' obsession is abroad filming two movies and therefore out of the public eye. During the end of 2008, and into 2009, Russell worked on *Get Him to the Greek* as well as an adaptation of Shakespeare's *The Tempest* (with Helen Mirren), and threw himself into stand-up comedy, recording a special for the USA and touring the UK, USA and Australia with his stand-up show *Scandalous*. He was also busy writing *Booky Wook 2*, a sequel to the first volume that would cover his relationship with Kate Moss and Sachsgate, and end with a very important date in his diary.

Russell Brand, BBC Radio bad-boy, lover of ladies and controversy, had once again been asked to present the MTV Video Music Awards. On 13 September 2009, he stepped out onto the stage at Radio City Music Hall, not knowing that the events of that night would lead to his second book's happy ending. It was, of course, on that night that he went out with Katy Perry for the first time, the woman who would just one year later become his wife.

'She's sleeping next to me now, tranquil and silently beguiling, it's impossible to ally her with the incandescent girl that blazes through the day,' he writes on the final page of *Booky Wook 2*, which is dedicated to her. 'She chose me, bottled me and cuffed me. And now this is my life, my girl, this beautiful woman.'

Both feisty and famous, the pair have a lot in common, as Katy realised one day early in their relationship. 'One night I picked him up from a meeting,' she told *Esquire* magazine. 'It was just me; I was in my gym clothes. I walked into the meeting – he had his stylist, his seamstress, his PR person, hair, make-up. I'm like "Oh my god, I am *you*. You are me." Two divas in one house. It's like splitting the atom – it shouldn't happen!'

8

Image and Style

Since pop music began it has been associated with style, fashion and image. Elvis Presley will always be remembered for the Vegas years, with his sideburns and his rhinestone-studded jumpsuits, while Michael Jackson's image, complete with sequined single white glove, is also famous throughout the world. The Beatles had their mop-top haircuts, followed by Sergeant Pepper gold-braided jackets, the Beach Boys will forever be associated with Hawaiian-style shirts, and Spandau Ballet for their New Romantic style of frilly shirts and floppy hair. Style often says just as much about an artist as their music does.

Of course, female pop singers have always handled style and image even better than the boys and the bands. You may not remember her music, but no one who saw it could ever forget punk singer Toyah's orange spiky hair and dramatic make-up, or Cher's revealing bodystocking and mass of curly black hair. The mistress of pop style, of course, was Madonna, whose changing looks influenced fashion for over a decade, from her 'Like a Virgin' lace corset and crucifix and pearls, to the bustier and leggings of 'Papa Don't Preach' and the conical bras designed by Jean-Paul Gaultier for her live performances. While Madonna broke the mould, changing her look and hair colour for every new album, there are many female artists who have followed her lead, Katy Perry being one of them.

Katy's look, of course, is very different to everyone else's. By the time she entered the pop charts, we were used to seeing Lily Allen, with her jet-black hair and prom dresses, Avril Lavigne with her skater-girl teen look, Gwen Stefani with her crop tops and platinum Jean Harlow-style hair, and Britney Spears with her tight clothes and blonde hair extensions. There was, of course, another striking artist on her way to fame whose style would be mentioned in newspaper pages around the world. But who would actually want to wear a dress made of plastic bubbles, or one made of meat, as Lady Gaga did?

The beauty of Katy's style, in comparison, is that it is fun and accessible. While some of her costumes can only be worn by a woman with a tiny figure like hers, many of the poppy, bright styles hark back to the fashions of the Fifties and Sixties and are ones that any woman could wear. But when you look at pictures and video footage from early on in Katy's career – when she was still Katy Hudson – there's little to indicate what a fashion icon she would go on to become. She was blonde, in jeans and shirts or frumpy dresses when she first sang live in Santa Barbara, and it was only after she started high school – and dyed her hair to its now-familiar black – that her unique sense of style began to emerge.

'I remember buying this fake leopard-skin coat that everyone at school laughed at but some of the really cool moms used to ask where I got it. That gave me a lot of confidence about my style,' Katy told *Grazia* magazine. In fact, a lot of her clothes in the early days of her career came from vintage shops and thrift stores, which explains her 'retro' look. 'I love shopping, like vintage shopping,' she told the *Star Scoop*. 'Not just going to a store, picking up clothes with labels or whatever. I love hunting, going to estate sales, and going to thrift stores, looking for antiques.'

She also grew more interested in fashion when she began dancing lessons as a teenager. 'When I first started out, I was really attracted to having my own sense of style because I started swing dancing, Lindy hop, and jitterbug. I would go to the Santa Barbara rec hall and I would learn how to dance there. I was taught by some of the more seasoned dancers who were actually very involved in the scene,' she told *Seventeen* magazine. 'These girls would get out of their old vintage Cadillacs with their pencil skirts and their tight little cardigans and their bullet bras and I thought it was so unique and different than what was going on in the 2000s. I love details. I love different colours. I love funny things. I have this one shirt that's got smiley faces as shoulders – so it's really cute and quite humorous. I love a good sense of humour in clothes.'

From early on, Katy wanted her style to reflect her personality – 'Very sassy, cheeky fun, cute, sexy and smart' – and her love of all things kitsch. After seeing Dominique Swain's outfits in the remake of *Lolita*, Katy was hooked, as she told *Times* journalist Sophie Harris: 'I was like, I wanna wear little jumpers! And rompers! And look like a pin-up! Is that OK?'

Her love of clothes even led her to the door of Universal Studios in Los Angeles – but, being Katy, she didn't exactly go in the front door. Instead, she would sneak in and pretend she was a stylist working there. 'I'd try on all the clothes, all these vintage gowns, and hope nobody would bust me,' she laughed while talking to journalist Rob Sheffield. 'I was a glamour ninja.' Certainly, being around all the Hollywood fashions did suit her style, and she took movie icon Jane Russell as one of her main influences.

Jane Russell was one of Hollywood's leading sex symbols in the 1940s and 1950s. Born in Minnesota in 1921, she began her career as a model before signing a seven-year contract with mogul Howard Hughes in 1940 when she was just nineteen. Her first movie role was in *The Outlaw*, and it made her instantly famous – and infamous – due to her impressive cleavage, which was prominently featured in the movie's poster (the image of her lying on a haystack became one of the most popular pin-ups for US servicemen during the Second World War), and led to the movie itself being censored and not properly released until 1946. (Hughes also commented that he invented the underwire bra for Jane's role in the movie, but in later interviews she stated that she didn't like it so wore her own bra instead.)

Like Rita Hayworth, Lana Turner and, later, Marilyn Monroe, Jane became known for her 'sweater girl' look (tight jumpers to emphasise the bust, basically), and her 38D-24-36 figure was also perfect for the halter-necked, full-skirted dresses and high-waisted shorts that were fashionable at the time.

'Jane Russell is the one I really copy,' Katy has said. And in an interview with *Time Out Chicago*, she explained that she had been lucky enough to meet the legendary star. 'I know Jane Russell, she's a friend of my family. I've tried to honour her. [My shorts] are as short as can be. I love the high-waisted thing. I wear jeans that hit me right at the waist because I got a small waist, big boobs and a butt. I try to stick to those features.'

By the time her first single, 'Ur So Gay', was released, Katy's image was well established – a mix of girly and sexy, sweet and sultry, bubblegum and burlesque. 'There are two people I really like and I probably borrow their style a little too much – Agyness Deyn and Dita Von Teese,' she told *Scarlet* magazine. 'I'm not strictly 1940s pin-up girl – I don't have that kind of dedication – so I give it a little twist. It's a little punk rock, a little *Lolita*, a little retro, a little Eighties. Just fun. It makes people smile I think.'

She has been compared to Betty Boop, Lucille Ball, Madonna and even drag queens ('Whenever anyone does my make-up, I say I want to be a couple of degrees away from being a drag queen,' she told the *Observer*'s Sheryl Garratt. 'I want fun on my face! None of this natural stuff.'), with a bit of tough-but-reverent chick mixed in, courtesy of a Jesus tattoo on her left wrist. 'I see it every time I'm playing guitar,' she said to Rob Sheffield. 'It's looking back up at me. That's where I come from, and probably where I'm going back to.'

And while she loves vintage clothes and thrift-shop finds, she also became a darling of fashion designers overnight. According to the *LA Times*, designers were calling Katy even before her first hit, having seen articles describing her as 'the next big thing' in newspapers and magazines. She caught the eye of quirky designer Betsey Johnson after wearing one of her designs for a photoshoot with *Women's Wear Daily* in the USA, and soon the designer was sending Katy dresses. 'Betsey really likes Katy's appearance,' said a Betsey Johnson spokesperson. 'She's very curvy and pin-up-girl-looking, a typical Betsey girl.'

One of the benefits of becoming a star was that people began to send gifts to Katy, in the hope she would wear them at important events where she would be photographed. 'Free clothes are one of my favourite things about life in the spotlight,' she laughed to Rebecca Nicholson of the *Observer*. 'People give me stuff, and I'm like – "I don't have to buy this?" I used to save up for this s*** all the time.' That said, Katy kept her own unique style once the cameras were on her: 'Some people feel under pressure to play the designer game, but I never do. I had many offers for the Grammys [in 2008], from people who offered to design a one-of-a-kind dress, but they couldn't pull off what I wanted, so I approached these new designers called The Blonds.'

David and Phillipe Blond, a.k.a. The Blonds, have, as *25* magazine described, 'been turning the fashion industry into a naughty freak show' since 2004. Before this, David was a window dresser for US department stores such as Macy's and Saks, while Phillipe was a make-up artist for MAC. Katy isn't their only celebrity fan – Rihanna, Fergie of the Black Eyed Peas and *American Idol* runner-up Adam Lambert have all been spotted wearing their distinctive hand-made designs and striking and jewelled prints. It was one of their designs that Katy wore in 2010 at the Victoria's Secret Fashion Show in New York, a mad floral corset that she teamed with a bubblegum mini-skirt and blue Louboutin heels.

Once she had become known for her quirky outfits – an electric-blue dress with eyes and eyelashes at the bust and a yellow sequined dress with Barack Obama's face on it for the 2008 MTV Europe Music Awards, a corset covered in fruit for the 2009 Grammys, for example – up-and-coming designers rushed to offer Katy their own unique designs. 'One girl contacted me on MySpace wanting to design for me,' Katy once said. 'I wear her costumes because they're so darn cute, like her pink romper with red glittering lips on the front of it. It doesn't matter what you wear on stage, so long as you sound good, but I love to go that extra jump.'

Her stage costumes are her most dramatic, be they corsets or fruit-adorned dresses, and she often has numerous dress changes during just one concert. 'When I get changed during a show it's like I'm at a Formula One pit stop,' she told *More* magazine. 'There's Velcro being ripped off and stuff getting strapped onto me. On one tour I wore a different outfit every single night. That was crazy, and not cheap. Of course, my friends totally loved it because they got to adopt my outfits after I was done with them.'

Even her outfits at home are eccentric. 'At home I sit around in a zebra-print romper suit from H&M,' she told the *Observer*'s Rebecca Nicholson. 'Rompers are very me. They're super-easy to run around in.'

'With anything you wear, it's about having confidence. A lot of people see me and think: she pulls off so many things that a lot of people can't pull off. It's fantastic to show off your personality through what you're wearing. You can give off an energy or a vibe just by wearing a silly, cute, light-hearted, smack-a-smile-on-your-face style. Why not?'

Katy's choices are often unusual, as she told *Scarlet* magazine. 'When I go somewhere that has a theme or a national colour, I wear it. I went to Japan dressed up in sushi! I'm just obnoxious like that – I'm so sorry.'

To help her in her quest for the perfect cute-but-sexy clothes, Katy has a personal stylist named Johnny Wujeck, and he is the one who has sourced some of her most memorable outfits, including the 'carousel dress' she wore at the Emmy Awards in 2009. 'Johnny saw it online and said "Oh my gosh, we've got to track that dress down. There's only one in the world and you have to wear it",' Katy told *Heat* magazine. 'So luckily we found it, but it was a little small because it was a sample size and I'm not a model. We had to sew some things in to make it bigger.'

Johnny clearly knows exactly what Katy likes. 'She loves sparkle and sequins. The Blonds is her perfect designer because that's exactly what they do,' he told *More* magazine. 'All their dresses are perfect for Katy. She wore one to the Kids' Choice Awards in 2010. We did a photoshoot the week before and she took the dress from the shoot and said: "I want to wear this for the awards next week." Her publicist was like, "Don't you think it's a bit 'booby' for a kids event?" But she wore it anyway!'

He also told *More* where Katy gets some of her clothes on the high street ('she loves high street shops like Topshop, ASOS.com and H&M and wears them with designer things'), and what she can't wear on her petite but curvy body: 'She can never usually wear backless dresses, but she wore a Zac Posen backless dress to the Grammy Awards [in 2010] and

pulled it off somehow. Katy loves her shape and loves showing it off! She can wear anything so long as it supports her
boobs. We haven't had any major fashion disasters, just zips
breaking all the time. We did a Christmas show where she
wore snowflakes and baubles but they kept falling off!'

Speaking of clothes falling off, Katy caused something of
a controversy when, in the summer of 2010, she posed top-
less for the cover of UK men's magazine *Esquire*. The pictures
were actually beautiful and tasteful, with Katy in corset-style
shorts and a crucifix necklace, hands covering her chest on
the cover, and photos of her inside in a black dress, long boots
and a low-cut leather halter-neck top. When *Cosmopolitan*
magazine asked her whether she had found the photoshoot
nerve-wracking, she replied: 'Mostly everyone on the set was
gay so it was totally fine. It was my idea. I mean, no one says:
"Oh Katy, you know you'll sell more records if you take your
top off." It's just me being a twenty-six-year-old young woman.
I'm confident in my skin I guess, lately.'

She continued: 'I take care of myself and also I think that
when you're in a supportive relationship you don't care anymore about outside. Things that maybe would have irked
you before don't matter because you found someone who
loves you no matter what. So I guess it's a mixture of, "Hey,
I'm twenty-six and I know these are my prime years and I
feel confident", and being loved-up.'

Her enviable figure was also displayed on the cover of
Rolling Stone magazine in the run-up to her October 2010
wedding, with some newspapers wondering whether Katy
had become too thin or had been airbrushed for the photos.
It was then revealed that she had adopted a strict regime

ahead of her big day. Katy, who had always gone to the gym regularly, was working out especially hard in the lead-up to her wedding, assisted by her personal fitness trainer Harley Pasternak: 'Her goal is to look amazing, always. She's getting in shape for everything . . . wedding, music videos, touring. She works out as often as she can, she's a busy woman but her goal is five times a week.'

Pasternak's 5-Factor Fitness programme is popular among celebrities, and Katy is certainly an example of how effective it is. It consists of a five-phase circuit of exercise that works each part of the body for five minutes, coupled with five small meals a day. 'A typical day's diet would be an egg-white omelet with a bowl of berries, an apple cinnamon smoothie, a chop salad, three-bean BBQ chips and finishing off with a seafood stir-fry for dinner,' says Pasternak.

His strict regime may work for Katy but she has admitted in the past that an egg-white omelet may not be her first choice for a yummy dinner. In 2009, she posted a photo of herself on Twitter in the bath, her modesty protected by a dinner tray with a partially eaten pizza on it, and when fans asked what her favourite food was, a diet omelet certainly wasn't on the list. 'Few of my fave things: BBQ chicken chop at CPK Chinese, chicken salad at Chinchins, Rock shrimp & yellow tail sashimi at Nobu, Crispy beef at Mr. Chow's, endive salad at Le Petite, four curry chicken salad at Urth Cafe, my beloved double double at INnOut.'

'Don't hate on Jack's Spicy Chicken sandwich! . . . I almost forgot . . . that damn crunch wrap supreme at Taco Bell. Okay that's all for now.'

And in case she wondered what such a diet would do for

her figure, a website called Worth1000.com posted a photo of what Katy would look like if she put on quite a few extra pounds. Katy posted the super-size photo on Twitter (captioning it 'Future Me') and was amused at the response. 'More people are saying "I'd still hit it" to the future me than the me now. Damn.'

Thin or super-curvy, it's Katy's bubbly personality and sense of style that makes her so attractive . . .

9

2010 – A Busy Year

A s September 2009 came to an end, tabloid journalists around the world continued to speculate about
Russell Brand and Katy Perry's surprise relationship. Katy,
meanwhile, had no time to sit down and read all that was
being written about her, because on 13 October she began
work on the album follow-up to *One of the Boys*.

Second albums (although, if you count *Katy Hudson*, this
was technically Katy's third) are often tricky, because artists
have to try and repeat the success of their first disc while
also delivering something new, so that the record appeals to
both long-time fans as well as attracting new listeners. 'The
second record is really important to me because I think it
shows whether I'm meant to do this, or I got lucky,' she told
Rolling Stone magazine.

'Basically what I want to do is not alienate the audience
that I have at all. I think some people feel like they have had
success with one thing and one idea and one record and they
want to pull a one-hundred-and-eighty and try a totally different thing,' she explained. 'I definitely feel like that's the
wrong move. I feel like you just have to grow from it, you

can branch off of it but keep the tree the same in some ways. Some people get full of themselves, and they think that anything they do is going to work or turn to gold or be the right move, and the reason why you're here is because of the people that like your music and the fans, so you always should keep an ear open to what they're saying.'

Knowing that she now had a name in pop, which enabled her to ask people to appear on her record, Katy told *Rolling Stone* that she wanted to work with names such as Calvin Harris (the Scottish singer-songwriter who has worked with Kylie Minogue and Dizzie Rascal) and Guy Sigsworth (the British songwriter and producer who co-wrote 'What It Feels Like for a Girl' with Madonna and 'Everytime' with Britney Spears), as well as Greg Wells, Dr Luke and Max Martin, who worked on *One of the Boys*. 'I guess I'm going to take the clout I have now and go, "Yeah, I want to work with you, because you wouldn't have worked with me five years ago",' she laughed.

The new album would have a different feel, although it would remain a pop record. She described the new sound she was aiming for as: '"Love Fool" by the Cardigans meets "Into the Groove" by Madonna but a little more meat on the bones lyrically. I'm not just gonna talk about the beat and just dancing, I like to get into the meaning.'

From 13 October, Katy spent most of her days recording in the studio. She would get up, go to the gym and then return home, then head off to the studio for the rest of the day before going home to bed and starting it all over again the next morning. While Calvin Harris turned out to be too busy to be able to work with her in the end ('We tried to make it happen but he got really famous so it didn't happen'), Katy and her team did line up a host of talented record producers and writers to help her with the sessions.

Katy hinted at some of the collaborators while she was recording the album: 'There might be some really cool guest appearances by some cool rappers from the West Coast. I mean, you'll just have to see, since I'm a California girl, you know. And then some best friends might be appearing . . . We'll see! It's going to be fun. It's going to be one of those records that is everybody's favourite guilty pleasure.'

One of the artists Katy was lucky enough to work with on the album was Thaddis 'Kuk' Harrell. He had worked on Beyoncé's hit 'Single Ladies (Put a Ring on It)', and also co-wrote Rihanna's smash hit 'Umbrella', so was a perfect choice to work on *Teenage Dream* (as the new album would be titled). She also drafted in Rivers Cuomo, of the band Weezer, and Ryan Tedder, who produced Beyoncé's album *I Am . . . Sasha Fierce*, and they all got started, working on one of the most hotly anticipated releases of 2010.

In between recording tracks, Katy was asked once again to present the MTV Europe Awards held on 5 November 2009 in Berlin. Katy began the evening by performing a cabaret-style medley of songs including the Black Eyed Peas' 'I Gotta Feeling', Kelly Rowland's 'When Love Takes Over', Kings of Leon's 'Use Somebody', Beyoncé's 'Halo' and Lady Gaga's 'Poker Face'. Clad in a burlesque corset and lace-up boots, behind an illuminated sign that stated we were present at the 'Katy Kat Club', it was another memorable opening act from her.

It was easy to see why MTV had invited her back. During

the course of the evening, Katy introduced Beyoncé's performance while wearing lingerie and a pink fuzzy stole, sitting in an oversized cocktail glass, and when Kanye West was mentioned in a nominations clip, she paused the video of him and jokingly interrupted him, getting her revenge on his now notorious interruption of Taylor Swift's acceptance speech at the MTV Video Music Awards.

Once again, she wore a series of distinctive outfits throughout the evening – a bustier and French knicker ensemble, a black outfit with pearls that she wore while reclining in a giant red sparkly stiletto shoe, a huge coral Viktor & Rolf prom gown with a big hole in the skirt, a bridal-style white gown and another black corset, this time with a red velvet jacket and hat. And just in case anyone was in any doubt as to whether Katy was dating Russell Brand, she confirmed it in a very public fashion . . . by wearing a basque in West Ham burgundy and blue colours (Brand's favourite football team) that also had Russell's Twitter name, Rusty, emblazoned on the back.

Brand was obviously pleased, as he wrote on his blog: 'Wow. Now my GIRLFRIEND has worn a West Ham basque while hosting the EMAs. What a day!' He also revealed he was going to take her to a game. 'Yes, I will be taking her to a game – West Ham v Everton,' he wrote. 'And, before it begins, no I won't be taking her up the Arsenal,' he added, showing that – while Katy may have caught his eye, she hadn't managed to tame his rude sense of humour.

Theirs was certainly a whirlwind romance. Their first date had been the night after the MTV Video Music Awards in September, because Katy had insisted that they go on a

proper date after their flirtation backstage. 'Can you imag-
ine the horrible feeling he had, when he was used to getting
everything he wanted?' she later told *Esquire* magazine.
Russell clearly realised he had met someone special, even on
that very first date – as well as giving her a copy of his autobiography, so that she knew what she was letting herself in
for, he also gave her a piece of jewellery. 'Russell gave me a
necklace on our very first date,' Katy told *Grazia* magazine.
'It's a Hindu hand of peace. But they're not beads [on it],
they're black diamonds. He gave me black diamonds on our
very first date! My hair was long and wavy at the time and he
kept calling me a mermaid. He opened the book and wrote
in it: "You're a mermaid and I'm drowning". Then he put the
necklace on me.' It obviously worked, as a week later Katy
and Russell jetted off on a holiday to Thailand together, with
Katy convinced that Russell had left his wild past behind
him.

'He was a heroin addict and now he's not. He was addict-
ed to all kinds of things and now he's not. And he basically
used to be a professional prostitute and now he's not,' she
told *Esquire*. 'He's an extremist, which can be both good and
bad. I always needed someone stronger than me and I am,
like, a f***ing strong elephant of a woman.'

By the end of their first month as a couple, the press
was following the pair when they were together and apart,
with tabloid journalists reporting on 6 October that the
relationship could already be over. 'After Russell Brand was
spotted taking two ladies back to his London pad, it seems
Katy Perry has decided to play him at his own game,' wrote
the *Daily Mail*. 'The US singer, who is said to be dating the

comic, was spotted out yesterday in Paris with a dapper gent on her arm.'

They were wrong, of course, as Katy's West Ham ensemble at the MTV Europe Awards proved a month later. By the end of November 2009, people who had doubted the relationship would last more than a week were surprised to hear that the romance was serious enough for Katy to take Russell to meet her mother and father. This was a big step, especially when you consider that Katy was introducing her strict religious parents to a former drug addict. Apparently, at their first meeting, Katy's dad Keith gave Russell a copy of his religious book *The Cry* . . . while Russell returned the favour by giving Keith a copy of his no-holds-barred autobiography *My Booky Wook*, featuring all the gory details of his life before Katy. It seems Katy's parents read it, too.

In an interview with the *Sun*, Katy's mum Mary said: 'Russell must go towards the light and not toward the darkness. Only God can take the very worst person and turn them around for good.' She added: 'You just have to see how the Lord's will is done. I mean, how many times have your kids disappointed you so profoundly you wanted to get up from the chair and knock them out? There are parts of Russell's book where he is hungry for positive influences in his life.'

Katy's parents went so far as to join Katy and Russell on a skiing holiday in Ischgl, Austria, where Katy was performing at the opening concert for the resort ('I really liked her parents, we got on well,' Russell told the *Daily Mail*. 'But I'm not sure if I want them coming on holiday with us all the time.'). And just a few weeks later, on the day before Christmas Eve, Katy and Russell were spotted sledging on Hampstead

Heath in North London, near Russell's home, and then at a carol concert at St. Paul's Cathedral that night, followed by a trip to the theatre to see *The Lion King*. Katy was even trying to master the differences between the English that Russell spoke and her American English, as she displayed on Twitter:

'Chips/crisps. Trash/bin. Trunk/boot. Bathroom/loo. Zebra/zahbra. Vitamins/vitaminz. Lady bug/lady bird. I need English lessons!'

Certainly, Russell was charmed with his American girlfriend. As she jetted off to spend Christmas Day with her family, rumours abounded in the press that the couple – together just four months – were on the brink of getting engaged. 'Russell knows Katy's the one for him,' a source told the *Daily Mail*. 'He's never been into a girl like he has with her and they're besotted. He asked her to marry him last week and she quickly said yes. Russell is searching for a jewellery designer to make up a ring in time for New Year after the pair discussed what they wanted to have.'

Russell had already made his feelings known in interviews earlier in December. 'I'd love to marry Katy – hopefully it's heading that way and I'm really happy,' he told the *Daily Mail*, while in another interview he described his pop-star girlfriend: 'She's amazing. I'm having a right laugh. She's a good person to spend time with and it's changed me – it's made me stop doing stuff that I probably shouldn't have been doing.'

Just before New Year's Eve, the loved-up couple headed to India for another holiday. On 30 December, Katy posted a photo of her and Russell on Twitter, featuring the pair of them hugging with the iconic Taj Mahal in the background. If the photo outside the most romantic building in the world didn't hint that an engagement was imminent, the news that Russell had put his London home on the market for £2.5 million, and that he had bought a house in Los Angeles for the two of them, from director Mark Romanek, certainly made it seem like a proposal was on the horizon.

It was an impressive house, too. Was it an engagement gift, as the tabloids hinted? A 1920s four-storey home in the scenic Hollywood suburb of Los Feliz, the house boasts four bedrooms, four bathrooms (one with spa bath tub), a 25m swimming pool, state-of-the-art kitchen, a living room, study and den, as well as seclusion due to a garden filled with beautiful trees. The top floor offers panoramic views of the surrounding area, which was once home to Walt Disney's first animation studio, and the couple would be able to see downtown LA from their bedroom. Neighbours included Charlie Sheen and Kristen Stewart, while Russell and Katy's local park is the famous Griffith Park, home of the Griffith Observatory featured in the James Dean-starring movie *Rebel Without a Cause*.

Certainly, it looked as though Russell was planning to propose. And on 6 January 2010 he confirmed what everyone had been guessing – that he had asked Katy to marry him. A publicist for Brand announced: 'We can confirm that Russell Brand and Katy Perry are engaged.' Details later appeared about how Russell proposed on New Year's Eve. According to a source at the hotel where they were staying, the five-star Taj Rambagh Palace, he took Katy to an ancient Indian fort during the day and bought her a traditional Indian dress there to wear out with him. They then took a horse-and-carriage ride to a garden where they enjoyed a romantic meal, and then rode on elephants to watch the New Year's Eve fireworks. After this, Russell took Katy to the Mughal garden at the hotel, where he had hidden an engagement ring for her amongst the flowers. He then went down on one knee and proposed.

'At midnight they enjoyed fireworks while sitting on an elephant, which Mr Brand specially requested. Then they were taken to the Mughal Garden – which was decorated by flowers and candlelight,' a hotel worker told the *Sun*. 'Mr Brand had given his butler the diamond ring to hide among the flowers. Miss Perry found it, he proposed, and she immediately said "Yes". After that they requested forty-five minutes' privacy. They looked like they were beautifully in love.'

Katy was thrilled, although the proposal was not as much of a surprise as Russell had hoped for. 'Unfortunately, I still Google myself sometimes,' she told radio host Ryan Seacrest. 'I saw [details of his proposal] on Google Alerts. I'm going to be honest.'

She told *Esquire* more about the proposal: 'Russell had a little turban on and we got into a horse and carriage which took us to this tent made out of tens of thousands of roses. Inside there was a stage show. Just before midnight, an elephant turned up – a painted elephant!'

Russell, meanwhile, joked about his proposal once it had appeared in the papers: 'There was an elephant involved and it was New Year's Eve. We were on an elephant just before it. We were in India. It was at midnight, and it is not a good idea to be on the back of an elephant during a fireworks display.'

The couple spent a few days enjoying the hospitality of the hotel. It is certainly a stunning place for a proposal – the Rambagh Palace is a former residence of the Maharajahs of Jaipur, nestled in 47 acres of gardens that have been described as the most beautiful in the world. There are courtyards with fountains, peacocks on the lawns, the Oriental Garden and the Mughal Garden – there's even an in-house astrologer. The hotel, voted the best in the world by *Conde Nast Traveller* magazine in 2009, has just over 100 rooms and suites, including the most luxurious, the Grand Presidential Suite, where Russell and Katy stayed. Filled with period furniture, the rooms of the suite are decorated with thousands of cut-glass pieces embedded in the walls and ceiling, which reflect the light from the crystal chandelier hanging above. If that wasn't decadent enough, the suite has a circular bed draped in gold fabric, and its own Jacuzzi.

Katy and Russell couldn't stay there forever, of course, as Katy still had her album to finish recording and Russell was filming scenes for his upcoming movie *Get Him to the Greek*. They returned to the UK, and on 10 January were spotted out shopping in Hampstead, London, near Russell's flat. There was nothing unusual about that, except that the paparazzi managed to take photos of the couple visiting a children's shop. A source told the *Sun* newspaper (of course): 'Russell and Katy had a wander around Hampstead. They visited children's shoe shop Cubs and had a lot of fun checking out all the little bootees. They then went to Café Rouge for a bit of lunch. Katy ordered scrambled eggs and asked for the eggs to be well done. And when Russell asked for a portion of chips she loudly announced to the waiter, "Hold the mayo."'

To the *Sun*, this was an indication that the newly engaged Katy was pregnant, since pregnant women are advised to avoid raw or undercooked eggs, and also not eat mayonnaise because it, too, contains uncooked eggs (which are considered a health risk to unborn babies). Could there be the patter of little Brand/Perry feet, the newspaper wondered?

Katy and Russell went so far as to fuel the rumours, maybe to show how daft they were. She posted several cryptic messages on Twitter – on 1 January: 'It's noon on Jan 1st here in the future, let me tell you 2010 is BUMPIN'!' She later sent a message via Twitter to Russell: 'I hear ur prego-ed.' Katy was even spotted visiting the doctor in Century City, Los Angeles, where it was speculated that she had had a sonogram. A few days later, a representative stated that she wasn't pregnant at all, and Katy posted another message on Twitter that left no one in any doubt. 'Ur gonna make me cry, maybe that's my period tho. THAT'S RIGHT I'M BLEEDING. Better luck next month, peepz.'

Within days it was time to jet off again. Katy and Russell headed to Los Angeles, and straight to an engagement party. Fifty of Katy's family and friends descended on Il Cielo restaurant in Beverly Hills to celebrate with the happy couple, where they were treated to champagne in the courtyard, which had been decorated with red roses and candles. They then sat down to dinner, which was finished off with a white chocolate cake decorated with the words 'Katy ♥ Russell'.

Katy arrived in LA just in time for the fifty-second Grammy Awards on 31 January 2010. She had been asked to present an award at the Staples Center event, and she was also nominated for Best Female Pop Performance for the song 'Hot n Cold'. 'It's nice to be nominated and I'm just happy to be recognised by the industry and by the group of people I have been working with for a long time,' she said on the red carpet. Clad in a skin-tight nude backless Zac Posen dress, covered in gold sequins, Katy presented an award with rock legend Alice Cooper, and posed on the red carpet with Russell, happily showing off her diamond engagement ring. She went home empty-handed, however (Beyoncé won Best Female Pop Performance for 'Halo'), while Beyoncé, Taylor Swift and Jason Mraz were the big winners of the evening. Katy's chart rival, Lady Gaga, had more nominations than Katy and went home with two Grammys, for Best Dance Recording for 'Poker Face' and Best Dance Album for *The Fame*.

Katy had lots to celebrate, though. Back in August 2009, it had been announced that she would be a guest judge on the US TV talent show *American Idol*, and the episode she appeared in was about to be broadcast ('I've seen this on TV so many times, I'm so excited!' she said when she accepted). Now in its ninth season, the series had always boasted Randy Jackson, Paula Abdul and Simon Cowell as the judges for the auditions and live shows, but on 5 August 2009, Paula Abdul had announced on Twitter that she was leaving the show. 'With sadness in my heart I've decided not to return to *Idol*,' she tweeted. 'I'll miss nurturing all the new talent, but most of all being a part of a show that I helped from day one become an international phenomenon.' People guessed that the reason Paula resigned was due to money negotiations, and also the addition of another judge, songwriter Kara DioGuardi, in Paula's final season. It seemed there was a judge's chair to fill, and with the auditions taping at various locations around the USA during the summer of 2009, it was decided to ask special guests to attend each of the first performances, when Simon, Randy and Kara would hear the good, the bad and the ugly, and decide who would be sent on to Hollywood, where the wannabe singers would eventually be whittled down to a top twelve.

Victoria Beckham, actor Neil Patrick Harris, singer Avril Lavigne and Joe Jonas of the Jonas Brothers were among those asked to attend the auditions and fill Paula's empty seat. Katy was asked to guest-judge in Los Angeles, and loved sitting and listening to the singers who performed in front of her. 'The *American Idol* experience was awesome,' she told *MTV News*. 'If I was offered that job as a permanent host, I would ditch my career and take on that career. *American Idol* was great fun. It was so easy. I didn't really make anybody cry, but I did tell the truth to some kids that might have needed to hear it.'

It didn't all go swimmingly. Katy clashed on air with fellow judge Kara DioGuardi when they debated who they should or shouldn't send through to the next round. Kara, who has written songs for Britney Spears, Kelly Clarkson, Pink and Kylie Minogue, teased Katy about her song 'I Kissed a Girl', changing the words to 'I kissed a dolphin' and in the end Katy said to her, 'Please stop, or I'll have to throw my Coke in your face.'

While it may have seemed that Katy couldn't take a joke, she soon proved she had a terrific sense of humour when she agreed to attend the Nickelodeon Kids' Choice Awards in March. Broadcast as a live show since 1988, the awards are voted for by children who watch the Nickelodeon TV Channels, and it's always the most fun of all the ceremonies held throughout the year. Children vote for their favourite movie, actor, actress, singers, shows and songs, there are live performances and lots of laughs – and also one thing the show has become notorious for . . . slime. Each year, at least one celebrity gets covered in gallons of green goo, either on or off the stage. Will Smith, 'N Sync, Tom Cruise, Pink, Jim Carrey, Johnny Depp, Sandra Bullock, Nicole Kidman and Harrison Ford are just some of the celebrities who have survived the slime, so being splattered with it was almost an honour, albeit a rather sticky one.

On 27 March, Katy attended the ceremony held at the UCLA Campus in Los Angeles. Hosted by comic actor Kevin James (from the TV series *King of Queens*), the show featured performances from Rihanna and Justin Bieber, while awards went to Taylor Lautner for his role in *Twilight: New Moon*, and to *Up* for best animated movie. In the music category, Taylor Swift won Best Singer and Best Song, while the Best Group award went to the Black Eyed Peas. Katy, dressed in a pretty yellow dress with blue flowers, and a matching bright blue wig, was due to present the award for Favourite Movie Actress, so she went up to the stage and opened a box that should have held the name of the winner. Instead, slime sprayed out from the box, completely coating Katy with such force that she actually fell over on the stage. Once covered, she went and hugged her co-presenter Jonah Hill, to make sure he got some slime on him too. 'I can't see anything!' she laughed as he got to announce that Miley Cyrus was the award winner. When she came to accept her award, Katy went to hug her and then backed away so that Miley didn't get slimed. 'Thank god we both wear wigs,' Miley joked. 'Thank you Katy, for not sliming me!'

By the end of April, Katy's new album was finished. There had been a late addition to the tracklist of the album, a song called 'California Gurls', which Katy wanted to be the first single. Capitol's Chris Anokute told HitQuarters.com: 'At 3 am, on the way back from an Oscar after-party, Katy texts me saying, "Chris, I don't think my record is done – there is one more song I want to write, I feel it in my gut! I want to write a song about California girls."' He remembers: 'At the time the Jay-Z song "Empire State of Mind" was huge and everyone in LA is singing, "New York . . . " and she wanted to have a song for California. She had the whole vision. I heard the demo and I was floored.'

Katy told *Rolling Stone* magazine where she got the idea from: 'It's so great that "Empire State of Mind" is huge and that everyone has the New York song, but what the f***? What about LA? What about California? It's been a while since we had a California song and especially from a girl's perspective. We took the references of Prince, which is always a great reference, and some of the '90s, almost house music references [for the song].'

Katy decided she wanted rapper Snoop Dogg to appear on the record with her. Chris called Snoop's manager, Ted Chung, and told him about the song and said it would be perfect for Snoop to appear on. However, Chung wanted to hear a demo of the song and there wasn't one for Chris to send him, so he suggested Chung come down to the recording studio to hear Katy sing it. The next thing Chris knows,

Chung is calling him back. 'I'm having dinner with my girl-friend and Ted calls me and says, "Snoop is in town, if you're at the studio we'll come now . . . " I get to the studio in a dash and Snoop beats me there. I see Katy Perry, [producers] Dr Luke and Max Martin's faces, and we look at each other like, "Oh my god!"'

Chris continues: 'He listens to "California Gurls" and then rolls up some magic and thirty minutes later we're listening to "California Gurls" featuring Snoop! To me that was a big moment – I've been listening to Snoop since I was a kid and to be able to play a role in getting one of the biggest rap artists on Katy Perry's single . . . wow, this is why I do this!'

The song was originally called 'California Girls', but Katy changed the spelling to 'Gurls' in homage to Alex Chilton, the lead singer of Big Star, who had released a song called 'September Gurls' in 1974. 'My manager, Bradford, he's from Mississippi, and he's a huge Big Star fan,' Katy told *Entertainment Weekly*. 'And with the death of one of their members, I had just written that song, and he's like, "Katy, just for me, will you please title it 'California Gurls', with a 'u'? People won't even know!" I don't know the whole catalogue of Big Star, but I did it because Bradford is one of my best friends, and I thought it was cool, and you know, the kids like those variations.'

It was a nice gesture. While casual rock/pop fans may not have heard of Alex or the band, rock aficionados know them well. Big Star was formed in Memphis in 1971, with Alex Chilton as lead singer, and they released pop/rock records in the same vein as The Kinks and The Byrds until they split in 1974. Regarded as 'the quintessential American power-pop band' and 'one of the most mythic and influential cult acts in all rock & roll' by allmusic.com, the band re-formed in 1993 and made the critically acclaimed album *In Space* in 2005, but sadly, Chilton died of a heart attack on 17 March 2010 after being taken to hospital feeling unwell earlier in the day.

Even with the spelling change, the name of Katy's song was very similar to a famous Beach Boys song. That wasn't a problem – but the Beach Boys' lawyers did take exception to the fact that, during his improvised rapping, Snoop Dogg actually says a line from the original song: 'I wish they all could be California girls . . . ' Legal representatives for the Beach Boys asked for them to be given a co-writing credit for the song, in addition to a portion of the royalties. 'Using the words or melody in a new song taken from an original work is not appropriate under any circumstances, particularly one as well known and iconic as "California Girls", Rondor, the Beach Boys' musical publishers, explained to *Entertainment Weekly*. 'It is up to the six writers and various publishers of "California Gurls" to decide whether they honour [our] claim or not.'

Surprisingly, while this was going on, two members of the Beach Boys admitted that they liked the song, with Brian Wilson calling it 'infectious' and Mike Love saying: 'The subject matter is still in vogue – just ask Katy Perry. I think the part she did is pretty cool. There are a lot of writers on it, and I think it's probably a stroke of genius to have the canine of cool, Mr Dogg, do his thing. But I think her creative part, her musical part, is pretty hooky. I think it brings the Beach Boys' 1965 classic to mind, that's for sure.'

Indeed, the boys themselves didn't seem as bothered as their music publishers, and by August, Mike Love emphatically stated: 'The Beach Boys are definitely not suing Katy Perry, we are flattered that her fantastically successful song is bringing to mind to millions of people our 1965 recording "California Girls".' Katy confirmed this on Twitter on 6 August: 'Just to be clear . . . no one is suing anyone,' she wrote. 'The press just loves to once again fabricate and exaggerate stories to get hits or sell papers.'

The summery single was due to be released on 25 May, but after clips of the song were leaked online, Katy's record company moved forward the release date to 7 May. With its catchy lyrics and cheeky pop feel ('so hot / we'll melt your popsicle . . . '), 'California Gurls' was an instant hit. As John Ivey, the programme director for LA's influential radio station KIIS FM said at the time: 'The impact [of the song] was immediate. The first day, we played it every hour.' The song became number one on iTunes instantly, sold more than one million downloads in four weeks and was top of *Billboard*'s Hot 100 chart within a month: 'For a record to get into power rotation [a hundred-plus plays per week] usually takes six-to-eight weeks. "California Gurls" took just thirteen days.'

The song received rave reviews, too. *USA Today* called it 'an effervescent toast to summer sun' while Digital Spy gave it five out of five stars and said it was 'as classy as the titular heroines' outfit of choice – "Daisy Dukes, bikinis on top" – but, thanks to an unstoppable pop chorus and Perry's charismatic vocals, just as easy to fall for. We mean, like, totally head over stilettos.' Of course, there was a memorable video to go with the smash hit song, too. Directed by Matthew

Cullen, one of the founders of animation and special-effects workshop Motion Theory (who also made Adele's 'Chasing Pavements' video), the look of the video was inspired by the art of Will Cotton, who served as art director on the shoot.

Will's paintings include the portrait of a naked Katy laying on a bed of cotton candy, and he is known for his elaborate landscapes made up of lollipops, marshmallows, whipped cream or cake, so it wasn't surprising to see that Katy's video had a similarly sugary feel. The video was shot on 15 May, with Snoop Dogg filming his cameo (in which he wears a suit covered in a cupcake design) the day before. Instead of setting the video on a Californian beach to tie in with the lyrics of the song, the video is set in 'Candyfornia'. 'It's a different world,' Katy told MTV. 'It's not just like, "Oh, let's go to the beach and throw a party and then shoot a music video!" It's more like, "Let's put us California Gurls in a whole different world!"'

The video opens with Snoop Dogg inviting us on a journey. We then see Katy, in a silver blue wig and candy-coloured dress, inside a candy-themed board game that he's playing, filled with candy canes, jelly babies, and even a gingerbread man in a gingerbread house. Katy also lies, nude, in a candy-floss cloud while she is singing and later dances and sings while wearing a bra made out of cupcakes. 'It's definitely something to watch when you have the munchies,' Katy added. 'It's all edible!' The video ends with Katy firing whipped cream from cans attached to her bra, and then sitting alongside Snoop, buried up to his neck in the California sand.

The song became so popular, it even made the headlines when – a few months later in October 2010 – a video of airline crew dancing to the song became a viral sensation. The staff of Cebu Pacific Airlines in the Philippines have always been known for their attempts to make air travel fun – they often present in-flight trivia games and quizzes – but they took things to a new level when they co-ordinated their in-flight safety demonstration to a mash-up of Katy's song 'California Gurls' and Lady Gaga's 'Let's Dance'. While the song played, the air hostesses danced in sync while demonstrating how to put on a life jacket and prepare for an emergency land-ing. The video, which ended up on YouTube, scored over six million hits in just five days. 'This actually surprised us,' said a spokesperson for the budget airline. 'It's overwhelming, we've seen a lot of positive response.'

Katy's instincts about the song had been proved right, and she had scored another massive hit. Her relationship with Russell Brand was going well, she was preparing to release her album . . . but there was just one tiny dark cloud amongst all the fluffy candy-coloured ones, it seemed.

Katy and Travis McCoy had experienced what seemed to be an amicable break-up before she started dating Russell, but out of the blue it seemed that her past relationship was coming back to haunt her. McCoy began giving interviews in which he talked openly about their break-up, and he also released a solo project that he said was inspired by Russell's movie *Forgetting Sarah Marshall*. McCoy told *Complex* magazine: 'I think [the project] was inspired by that whole situation. At the end of the day, I think anyone who has been through some s*** can relate to [the music]. It could have been about my girlfriends before, but I'm [going to] keep it real with you, it was definitely about Katy Perry. I definitely felt a certain way about the whole situation. Having a year and a half to reflect on it, you start questioning everything…'

He continued: 'The timelines . . . she got engaged so quickly after. I was like, "Really?" I had to sit back and reassess what was really going on. After you have some time to start thinking about it, you start putting things together. I'm over it.' While the pair are no longer in touch, McCoy was certain that Katy knew about his project. 'I'm sure she knows. The mix tape is not airing out any dirty laundry. If anything, it's me poking fun at myself. If you've seen *Forgetting Sarah Marshall*, that's my life. I'm that dude.'

In fact, he later went so far as to name the mix tape *Forgetting Katy Perry* – just in case anyone was unsure who it was about. And while the tape was an unofficial release of Travis's, he made sure to have one last mention of their relationship when he released his solo album a few months later, in July. The last track on *Lazarus* is called 'Don't Pretend', and he told reporters what it was about: 'That song is the most introspective and personal on the album. In a sense, I felt I'd had my heart ripped out. I'm crying throughout the song. The album is about coming out the other side of something really painful . . . there was a lot of stuff that didn't make the album because it was too dark.'

Luckily, Katy didn't have time to dwell on Travis's comments about their former relationship. As well as promoting her own single, 'California Gurls', she was there for Russell as he began interviews and press trips to discuss his first leading role as an actor in the movie *Get Him to the Greek*. Russell reprised the role of obnoxious pop star Aldous Snow that he had first performed in the movie *Forgetting Sarah Marshall*, and in this movie, Aldous has hit rock bottom. After his girl-friend leaves him, taking their son, and his album is a flop, he takes comfort in lots of drink and drugs. Meanwhile a young employee at Aldous's record label, Aaron Green (played by Jonah Hill), gets the unfortunate job of going to London to find the sozzled Aldous and then bring him back to Los Angeles in time to perform a concert at the Greek Theater's tenth anniversary.

It is, of course, a trip fraught with disaster as Aldous drinks, attempts to smuggle drugs, romances every woman in his path and generally causes complete chaos en route to Los Angeles. Along the way, his character meets some real-life music stars including Pharrell, Metallica's Lars Ulrich, Pink and Christina Aguilera . . . but Katy's cameo role didn't make the final movie.

The scene Katy had filmed back in 2009 – before the two had even considered dating – had her smooching Russell, but it was left out of the film. When the movie was due to be released, Russell confessed to MTV: 'I've not asked [what happened to the scene] because it's slightly awkward, nor have I told her [she's been cut from the movie]. I think it might be because it would seem kind of cheesy to have her and I in the movie together.'

Katy didn't mind, and she accompanied Russell to the movie's premiere in Los Angeles on 26 May. He wore a white suit and shirt with gold boots and rock-star shades, while Katy dazzled in a silver metallic dress, split to the thigh and boasting a train. It was then off to the MTV Movie Awards a few days later, on 6 June, where Katy joked about her role ending up on the cutting room floor.

'It got cut!' she laughed to *MTV News*. 'I was like, "I'm sleeping with you, and you're not gonna put me in the movie? That's so messed up!"' Getting more serious, she chatted about why she didn't mind her role being removed from the final film. 'It seemed too much of a literal movie then, which I totally understand from a director's perspective or from a moviegoer's [perspective],' she said. 'If you saw me and Russell making out, although it'd be cute to, 'cause that was the first moment we met, [it would be like,] "There's Russell Brand in the movie," not Aldous Snow, and they want it to be Aldous Snow, [so it's] completely understandable.'

Katy and Russell both appeared on the same stage, at least (although not at the same time) at the MTV Movie Awards in Los Angeles. Russell presented the award for Breakthrough Performance, alongside his *Get Him to the Greek* co-stars Jonah Hill and P. Diddy, while Katy performed 'California Gurls' with Snoop Dogg. She started the performance above a large flashing 'California' sign on the wall, suspended on a surf board that was lowered onto the stage. Snoop Dogg later joined her (he came in on a moving throne) while lots of beach balls were released into the audience. Not missing a trick, the MTV cameras found Russell in the audience (not difficult, when he was wearing that bright white suit) and filmed him dancing away to his fiancée's performance.

It was then off to Russell's home town of London for a few days, before Katy headed off to Dublin for another TV performance – this time on Britain's *The X Factor*. During the summer filming of the auditions for the 2010 series of *The X Factor*, one of the judges, Dannii Minogue, was heavily pregnant and wasn't able to attend. Rather than have only three judges debating the merits of the auditioning public, Simon Cowell decided to copy what he had done for *American Idol* earlier in the year – ask well-known celebrities to fill Dannii's empty chair during the audition process. Katy's performance on *American Idol* had gone very well, so Simon asked Katy if she would come and judge during one day of the auditions.

Katy joined Simon, Cheryl Cole and Louis Walsh at the June auditions in Dublin. ITV.com asked her what she was looking for in the contestants: 'I wanted to find someone that has a spark that is different and unlike anything that is already out there. The industry is really competitive and so I was looking for someone not only with a voice, but maybe with a distinct voice to them. I can't wait to see some kind of diamond in the rough; that would be so fantastic!'

She also chatted about what kind of judge she thought she would make: 'I'm definitely not going to be a sugar-coated judge, just because there are people that need advice and they need criticism and sometimes they need to hear the truth,' she said on the day. 'If it's obviously not going to work out for them, ever, and they haven't figured that out, they need to aspire to something else. It's a bit of a hard thing to do, to tell someone that hard truth but hopefully I can say it in a way that isn't a mean way, but just a helpful way. Because I want people to fulfil their dreams and their goals, but you know, if you can't dance, don't dance!'

On her way to the auditions, Katy was clearly thrilled to be meeting her fellow judges. 'I love Simon! I've met him a few times before on different chat-shows and he's very confident and very sarcastic, which is definitely my cup of tea.

I love Cheryl, she's a fashion inspiration, of course, and I want those dimples, right there. And, Louis, I had never met, but I was excited to meet him in his home town. I'm just excited to be in that great company.'

After the auditions were over, Katy headed back to the USA to work on her next single release, but she revealed on comedian Alan Carr's chat-show just how much she had enjoyed the *X Factor* experience, and working with one judge in particular: 'I adore Cheryl, she's amazing. I'm very happy with my own English stud but if I wasn't with him I'd be trying to date Cheryl. Nobody should be as beautiful as she is. I know people get turned on by Simon's power but if I was single, I'd rather sleep with Cheryl than Simon!'

Fans had to wait until the end of August for Katy's appearance on *The X Factor* to be broadcast, but in the meantime she was busy working on her second single from her upcoming album. 'Teenage Dream' was the song (and the title of the album), and it was released on 23 July. The song was composed by Katy and Bonnie McKee who had already co-written 'California Gurls', but it wasn't the easiest one to work on. The pair wanted to write a song about being a teenager, as Bonnie explained to interviewer Alex Kazemi: 'Katy and I wrote and rewrote this song four times,' she remembered. 'It started off being kind of a "forever young" idea. That was always the spirit of it. Katy started with a lyric about Peter Pan that was cool, but it just kept feeling too young, and we wanted it to have more edge, more sex. There was a version that included a line that said, "And the next thing you know, you're a mom in a minivan", that kept us laughing uncontrollably for an hour. We literally wrote it front to back three times and were rolling around on the studio floor delirious.'

Katy and Bonnie tried other versions, but nothing was working. In the end, Bonnie went home and thought about the song and what it should be about: 'I thought about my own adolescent years, my own first love. I thought about watching Baz Luhrmann's *Romeo + Juliet* and putting on a little mini disco ball light and just dreaming of Leo [DiCaprio]. I thought about me and my friends sitting around at slumber parties in the '90s, giddy even just THINKING about boys. Back when love and sex were still mysterious and magical.'

In the end, Bonnie came up with a chorus, while Katy worked on the verses that told a story about being in love and being a teenager again. As Katy told MTV: 'I wrote that song in Santa Barbara and it was a very pure moment for me, because that's where I'm from. And it was, like, where I started my creative juices. And also it kind of exudes this euphoric feeling because everybody remembers what their teenage dreams were – all the girls that were on your poster walls. And I want to continue to be one of those . . . teenage wet dreams,' she laughed.

The song was also about Katy's own journey from teenage singer to adult pop star, complete with fiancé. 'It is about someone making you feel like you are having that teenage dream about someone,' she told the *Daily Record*. 'Like when you are in high school and you dream about that person you want to make out with or date. To me, this year is pretty heavy. I am going to be getting married and putting out this record, and there is so much going on that it's nice to think of those young dreams.'

The song was another hit, and there was, of course, a

video to match. Directed by Yoann Lemoine, who had worked on videos for Moby, and filmed in Katy's home town of Santa Barbara, the video features cameo performances from some of her old friends and has Katy driving along a California road with her 'boyfriend', going to a beach party and ending up in a motel. 'I had to make out with a boy, which was very traumatising; I was kind of mean to him,' Katy said on YouTube about the filming. 'I would be the one to call cut because I was like, "Oh I can't do this!", I feel so horrible. But I know it's a job. We [she and Russell] understand what our work is.'

The single was quickly followed by the release of Katy's album, also called *Teenage Dream*, which came out on 24 August. The album went straight to number one in the USA, and featured a Will Cotton photo of Katy lying on a puffy pink cotton candy cloud on the cover. Katy even asked that the CD be made to smell of candyfloss, so the booklet inside was spritzed with it. 'It actually smells a bit like My Little Pony,' she told the *Guardian*. 'You know, the toys? So it smells of your childhood, which is always endearing.'

The tracks on the album were again all written or co-written by Katy. *Teenage Dream* kicks off with the title song, and is then followed by:

★ 'Last Friday night (T.G.I.F.)' – in which she sings about getting drunk and dancing on table-tops
★ 'California Gurls' – the album's first smash-hit single
★ 'Firework' – which was to be the next single off the album
★ 'Peacock' – a racy song that infuriated reviewers with its lyrics, this track begins with Katy chanting 'I want to see your peacock, cock, cock'

★ 'Circle the Drain' – which many assumed to be about Travis McCoy with its lyrics: 'Thought I was the exception / I could rewrite your addiction / You could have been the greatest / But you'd rather get wasted / You fall asleep during foreplay . . .'

★ 'The One That Got Away' – a song about the teenage boyfriend she let get away

★ 'E.T.' – 'You're so hypnotising / Could you be the devil? / Could you be an angel?' sings Katy in a song rumoured to be about Russell Brand

★ 'Who Am I Living For?' – a ballad about spirituality and faith

★ 'Pearl' – one of the last songs Katy wrote for the album, about a strong woman held back by her man

★ 'Hummingbird Beat' – the bouncy song about being in love, again inspired by Russell Brand

★ 'Not Like the Movies' – in which Katy sings about the perfect love.

This time around, the album brought Katy some mixed reviews. One of the first comments came from a familiar source, her ex, Travis McCoy. He talked to MTV about the song 'Circle the Drain', which was rumoured to be about him. 'I heard she put out a song that's about me, or about some old habits or whatever. I look at it like this: I'm just stoked that she finally has a song with some substance on her record. Good job.'

Professional critics disagreed about whether the album was great or not. allmusic.com said 'Once again, the music feels familiar, so Perry distinguishes herself through desperate vulgarity', while *Spin* magazine commented '*Teenage Dream* won't disappoint parents looking for reasons to worry about their kids.' *Entertainment Weekly* was more positive: 'When she is good, she is very, very good . . .', while *USA Today* gave it three out of four stars. Katy's fans loved it, however, and the album sold a whopping 192,000 copies in the USA in its first week of release. It topped the Canadian, UK and Australian album charts, too, and quickly became one of Europe's bestselling albums of the entire year.

Katy only had a few days to enjoy the album's success before she was off to the 2010 MTV Video Music Awards, which were held at the Nokia Theater in Los Angeles. Since Katy had spent much of the year that MTV covered in their awards in the studio, only the first single taken from *Teenage Dreams*, 'California Gurls', was eligible for any of the awards, and Katy found herself nominated for two – Best Female Video and Best Pop Video. Unfortunately, she lost both to Lady Gaga (for her video to 'Bad Romance'), who dominated the evening. Gaga had received an impressive thirteen nominations for her hits 'Bad Romance' and 'Telephone' (which was a duet with Beyoncé), and she won eight of the awards. No stranger to controversy, Lady Gaga also became the talking point of the night when she accepted her award for Video of the Year wearing a dress, hat and shoes made from raw meat. PETA president Ingrid Newkirk wondered whether it was real meat, suggesting the dress 'would smell like rotting flesh and likely be crawling in maggots', while the designer of the dress, Franc Fernandez, said the meat was clean and strong and actually dried out under the stage lights ('it becomes jerky').

In contrast, Katy kept a relatively low profile at the awards, in an elegant black and white Marchesa dress, with Russell's face painted on her fingernails. It seemed that being engaged to Russell had tamed her, but it wasn't long, however, before her own choice of dress made headlines around the world.

Katy was continually in demand throughout 2010 – if she wasn't listening to young wannabes auditioning for *The X Factor*, she was performing her latest single at an awards ceremony. If she wasn't being interviewed on TV somewhere in the world, she was being photographed with Russell house-hunting, wedding-planning or simply going out to dinner. It is exhausting to read every single thing written about Katy during that busy year, so it must have been even more tiring for her to be living it!

One request, though, was just too much fun for Katy to turn down, despite how busy she was in the run up to her October 2010 wedding. The makers of children's TV show *Sesame Street* called Katy to ask her if she would like to be a celebrity guest on the programme, and she didn't hesitate to say yes.

Sesame Street is no longer shown in the UK, which is a terrible shame, but it is still a huge hit in the USA, and is also broadcast around the world. By 2001, more than 120 million children were watching the show in 140 countries. There have been over 4,000 episodes since it began in 1969, and the puppet characters that live on Sesame Street itself are famous throughout the world. Even if you have never seen an episode, or watched one of the *Sesame Street* movies, you'll recognise the characters from kids' clothes, toys and bedding – Oscar the Grouch (the mushy-green-coloured grump who lives in a garbage can), bright-yellow Big Bird, pals Bert and Ernie, and cheeky little red monster Elmo.

Over the forty-something years that *Sesame Street* has been on TV, celebrities from film, TV and music have lined up to be asked on as guests, so Katy's invitation was a special mark of her rising fame. She would be joining a very impressive list of people who have laughed, joked and sung alongside the cute puppets including (to name just a few): astronaut Buzz Aldrin (who answers Cookie Monster's question about whether the moon is actually a big cookie), David Beckham (who acted out the word 'persistent' with Elmo), C-3P0 and R2-D2 from *Star Wars*, Hillary Clinton, Robert De Niro (who explained what an actor was to Elmo, and then impersonated him), Michael Jackson, Julia Roberts and First Lady Michelle Obama (who teaches children about growing vegetables).

Katy was asked to join this illustrious group for an episode of the forty-first season of *Sesame Street*, which would be broadcast in the USA on New Year's Eve 2010. Like many stars before her, Katy was to adapt one of her hit songs for the show, which she would perform with one of the *Street*'s famous puppets. Katy chose her hit song 'Hot n Cold', and was asked if she would like to sing it with loveable Elmo.

In the scene she filmed, Katy appears in a lime metallic dress, with a veil and flowers in her hair, and asks Elmo if they can play dress-up. But the cheeky red monster runs away, and Katy sings 'Hot n Cold' while she chases him, trying to get him to play with her. It's great fun, but when the producers of *Sesame Street* released the clip to YouTube, a problem arose.

While Katy's outfit wasn't remotely as shocking as some of the costumes she has worn on TV and on stage before, the top half of her dress was quite revealing – a corset-style bodice (with nude mesh to her neck) that showed a bit of her famous cleavage. Presumably, the makers of *Sesame Street* thought her attire was suitable enough, as they had filmed her without asking her to change her outfit, but when the clip aired on YouTube, parents took to the Comments section of the site in their droves, proclaiming that Katy's outfit was just too hot for children's TV.

'I think she should have covered those tits a little more for a children's show,' commented one, while another added, 'This woman can't even go on a children's show without her boobs hanging out!' Not everyone was complaining, however, as over a million views were counted of the clip before *Sesame Street*'s producers removed it from the site. Sesame Workshop, the makers of the show, released a statement: '*Sesame Street* has a long history of working with celebrities across all genres, including athletes, actors, musicians and artists. *Sesame Street* has always been written on two levels, for the child and adult. We use parodies and celebrity segments to interest adults in the show because we know a child learns best when co-viewing with a parent or caregiver. We also value our viewers' opinions and particularly those of parents. In light of the feedback we have received on the Katy Perry music video which was released on YouTube only, we have decided we will not air the segment on the television broadcast of *Sesame Street*, which is aimed at preschoolers.'

Katy, happily, wasn't fazed by this turn of events. When asked about the controversy, she just tweeted 'Wow, looks like my play date with Elmo has been cut short!' while husband-to-be Russell, spoofing the way each episode of *Sesame Street* ends by revealing the number and letter that were featured on the show, tweeted back 'Today's *Sesame Street* will NOT be brought to you by the number 34 or the letter D.'

She also managed to turn what could have been an embarrassing controversy into a fun one, as only Katy could. Just four days after the news broke of her risqué outfit on 23 September, she appeared in New York on comedy sketch show *Saturday Night Live* wearing a teeny-tiny red Elmo T-shirt, cut at the neckline to expose her bust. With her hair in bunches, and wearing glasses, she pretended to be a volunteer librarian named Maureen who is stunned by the attention she is getting at work due to a growth spurt.

It's a very funny sketch, and one that showcased Katy's sense of humour. Things were about to get more serious for her, however, as unbeknownst to the press, Katy and Russell were putting together the final preparations for a very important day that was just a few short weeks away – their wedding . . .

10

Will You Take This Comedian . . . ?

The marriage of an American pop princess to a controversial British comedian was never going to be a conventional one. There would be no popping along to Marylebone Registry Office for this pair, whose very romance had surprised their fans, and whose relationship has unfolded in the spotlight. Instead, nine months after Russell Brand's romantic proposal to Katy in India, he and his bride-to-be – and around eighty-five guests – headed back to the subcontinent in October 2010 for their much-anticipated wedding.

Why did the pair decide to marry in India? *Hello* suggested that Katy and Russell had been inspired by the magazine's coverage of Elizabeth Hurley and Arun Nayar's wedding there three years earlier, reporting that a friend of Katy's had said: 'She loved the Elizabeth Hurley wedding pictures because she thought it was colourful, camp and very in keeping with her and Russell's spiritual and philosophical beliefs – plus it gives her lots of opportunities for costume changes!' (One hopes the similarities end there – Elizabeth and Arun have since announced they have separated.)

The venue the pair chose for their ceremony was the exotic Aman-i-Khás hotel, near a tiger sanctuary at Ranthambore National Park in Rajasthan, three hours from Jaipur. Described as a 'wilderness camp' of ten luxurious tents, it is surrounded by the Aravalli hills and boasts a spa, organic garden and pool for its extra-special guests. The air-conditioned tents themselves are more like luxury suites, with cotton drapes separating each one into rooms – a bedroom, lounge area, bathroom and dressing room, which can be yours for around £600 a night.

Knowing that the world was watching them, Katy and Russell couldn't have picked a better, more private spot – but just in case the paparazzi descended, they also booked into four hotels in Jaipur itself, including the Rambagh Palace where the pair had been staying when Russell proposed on New Year's Eve 2009, and where many newspapers expected the actual wedding to be.

They also didn't tell anyone – even their guests – exactly when the ceremony was going to take place. Invitations were sent out during the summer, asking guests to keep free the entire week of 18–25 October, and giving them all enough time to arrange the vaccinations and tourist visas that are required for travel to India.

In the weeks prior to the wedding, rumours abounded in the press. Russell was apparently going to charter a private plane to fly out most of the guests to the wedding. Celebrity-wedding-planner Mindy Weiss – who organised the weddings of Gwen Stefani and Gavin Rossdale, and Charlie Sheen and Denise Richards – had reportedly been hired by the pair. Katy was going to ride into the wedding venue atop an elephant. Elie Saab would design her gown . . . or one of them, as the rumour mill suggested there would be at least six 'wedding dresses' for the blushing bride. But, despite this being recognised as the celebrity wedding of the year – and numerous reporters being sent to Heathrow and airports in India to follow the pair – Katy and Russell managed against all odds to keep many of the details to themselves.

Would there be alcohol at the celebrations (Russell being a reformed drug addict, sober for over seven years)? Would Katy's wedding attire be revealing enough to offend Indians or would she tone down her racy fashion for this important day? The paparazzi kept on guessing – as did Russell, admitting that he was leaving much of the planning to his bride. 'The bride is in charge,' he said to reporters. 'So you initially think, "Oh, I'll just say yes to everything that they ask." But that's not enough. You have to be interested, *then* say yes.'

Even with Katy's meticulous planning, there were some bumps in the road on the way to the altar. First, Katy let slip something very interesting during an interview with Graham Norton in June 2010. Talking about Russell, she said: 'Life's never dull with him; that's why I married him!' The audience gasped, wondering whether this meant the couple was already secretly hitched. Katy quickly corrected herself. 'That's why I'm *marrying* him,' she smiled. She also referred to Russell's mother as her mother-in-law, but denied that a wedding had taken place.

Then, Katy's pal, singer Rihanna, let slip where the actual nuptials were taking place. She told a US radio DJ that she had her work cut out for her, planning a hen night for her friend with a theme to tie in with an Indian wedding. 'How do I match that?' she asked, accidentally revealing the pair's plans to marry in the same country where Russell had proposed.

Rihanna had become a great friend during Katy's rise to pop stardom, and one thing they had in common was their drive to become a recording artist from an early age. Born in Barbados in 1988 to Guyanan and Barbadian-Irish parents, Robyn Rihanna Fenty began singing at the age of seven, and by fifteen had formed a singing group with two school friends. They got to audition for producer Evan Rogers, who had also worked with Christina Aguilera, who was on holiday in Barbados at the time, and when he heard Rihanna singing Destiny's Child's cover of 'Emotion', he decided to work with her. At just sixteen years old, Rihanna travelled with her mother to Rogers's home in Connecticut and stayed with him and his wife while she recorded a demo to send to record companies.

Def Jam executives heard the demo, and a year after she came to the USA, Rihanna was signed by the label's then-president, Jay-Z. Her debut single, 'Pon de Replay', was released in August 2005, around the same time Katy was trying to get signed to a record label in Los Angeles. It became a hit, and was followed by Rihanna's first album, *Music of the Sun*, which sold well but received mixed reviews. Undeterred, Rihanna returned to the studio straight away to record a second album, which was released in April 2006, and boasted two hit singles.

While Rihanna tried to change her sound for her third album in the hope that it would send her career into the stratosphere, Katy's career was also on the rise, having just signed with Capitol Records. When she was recording tracks such as 'Ur So Gay' for a release in 2008, Rihanna was working on her third album *Good Girl Gone Bad*, which came out in the spring of 2007. Recording with names such as Timbaland and will.i.am, this was to be the album that changed Rihanna's career, for it contained the song 'Umbrella', which spent ten weeks at number one in the UK and also won Rihanna the Monster Single of the Year and Video of the Year at the MTV Video Music Awards in 2007.

By 2008, Katy's and Rihanna's paths had begun to cross at events around the world. They were due to share the stage at the 2009 Grammy Awards, but Rihanna cancelled her appearance at the last minute – of course, by the next day everyone knew why when news stories appeared of her boyfriend, Chris Brown, being arrested for physically abusing her. Despite this awful event, her star continued to rise, however, and both she and Katy often found themselves at the same awards ceremonies, performing and winning (and being nominated) for similar awards.

Both young women who love to perform, love to have fun, and work incredibly hard, it is hardly surprising that they became friends – and that Katy picked Rihanna to be part of her hen night and her wedding. She chose well as the hen night that Rihanna put together was a huge success – she arranged for a stretch Hummer car to whisk Katy and twenty-five pals to see Cirque du Soleil in Las Vegas, followed by a boozy trip to a strip club in the city that left Katy joking that she needed to 'sign up for a liver transplant'.

Meanwhile, Russell had a tamer evening in London on

26 September. First, he and his pals watched West Ham beat Tottenham Hotspur 1–0, before visiting the Albany pub near Regent's Park and then ending up at one of Peter Stringfellow's clubs, Angels. 'It was the most sober stag night in the history of nightclubs,' Stringfellow himself commented, while Russell told *Heat* magazine 'I don't take drugs anymore, I don't drink – so what do you do? I can't have sex with people on the stag night, so what's the point? I might as well watch television! That's the challenge for my best man, Nik [Linnen, his manager] – to make a stag night for a man who can't have sex, do drugs or drink in any way.' And despite having rowdy pals such as Jonathan Ross, Noel Gallagher, Carl Barât and David Baddiel along for the fun, it seems Russell behaved himself . . . and was tucked up in bed (alone) by 2 a.m.!

Unfortunately, not everything went as smoothly in the run-up to the wedding. Just a few weeks before the big day, Russell and Katy were at Los Angeles International Airport waiting to board a flight when Brand was arrested for pushing a photographer. Snapper Marcello Volpe was allegedly trying to take a photo up Katy's skirt when Russell shoved him, and the British comedian was arrested on suspicion of battery – a charge that could have resulted in him being banned from visiting the USA in the future.

Clearly angry at this turn of events – and the possibility that they would have to delay their wedding if Russell was found guilty – Katy tweeted 'If you cross the line & try to put a lens up my dress, my fiancé will do his job & protect me. Stand by your man. Don't f*** with the Brands.' Russell was taken into custody but released when he posted a $20,000 bail, while back in England his pal Jonathan Ross joked on Twitter 'I am currently baking a cake with a file and hacksaw in it for my dear friend Russell.'

Even Russell himself saw the humour in this strange and unexpected situation, tweeting to his fans: 'Thanks for all your sweet messages of support. After the tips I picked up in chokey I'm an infinitely more proficient criminal.'

Happily, prosecutors in Los Angeles eventually decided not to press charges. On 8 October, Los Angeles City Attorney's Office spokesman Frank Mateljan announced: 'Based on the information, it has been determined that this is the most appropriate action at this time,' adding that Russell Brand would simply receive a reprimand from a California judge on 19 November 2010 – a few weeks after his and Katy's planned nuptials. Phew!

After last-minute plans were put into place, the pair jetted off to India with the press in hot pursuit, and arrived at Jaipur Airport on Wednesday, 20 October, covering their faces from the waiting snappers – but not before a photo was taken of Katy sporting a traditional Indian nose ring known as a nath, that featured a pretty chain running across her right cheek and fastened to her ear. The ring symbolises a bride-to-be's purity, and is worn on the wedding day until the groom removes it at the end of the festivities.

Katy's parents arrived later in the day, following the happy couple's arrival, as did Russell's mum Barbara. Katy, knowing that all eyes were on her, tweeted: 'Greatest gift u can give us is respect & ♥ during this private time.'

Despite her hopeful wish, trouble was once again on the horizon for the couple. Settled into their wilderness camp, Russell and pal David Baddiel decided to go on a pre-wedding safari in the nearby Ranthambore National Park. However, their peaceful trip was ruined by four local photographers following them in a jeep, and before long things had escalated into a heated row. The *Sun* newspaper reported that one of Russell's bodyguards attacked the cameramen, first punching the driver and grabbing his keys, and then hitting two of the other snappers. The security men returned to Russell and David's car and drove off, leaving the photographers stranded. It must have been a scary time for the cameramen, as they were in the middle of a tiger sanctuary where there had been four recent tiger attacks.

Luckily, park rangers retrieved the keys from Russell's minders within minutes and escorted the men to safety. They made a complaint to the local police, and a source for the *Sun* reported that when Russell returned to the resort, he 'came back from the safari, almost in tears. He grabbed Katy and they went straight to their room. His team were more than a little heavy-handed.' Later that day, the bodyguard in question went to the police and apologised, and no arrests were made.

Each day, more reports and speculation appeared in the press, including the news that the couple were already married! Three days before the wedding, numerous websites showed photos of Russell wearing what looked like a wedding ring, although when questioned he remarked it was just his 'favourite piece of jewellery'.

Guests continued to arrive at the resort, but there was one noticeable absence. Katy's close friend Rihanna, who had organised her hen do, was unable to attend the wedding.

A source close to the star explained to *Us* magazine, 'Rih was finishing her album, and she just switched managers, so she had to pull out at the last minute. It was always sort of up in the air that she would go anyway, and Katy knew that. They saved her a room just in case, but they always knew it would be nearly impossible for her to make it as she's still finishing the album and it's out in a few weeks.'

The press had a field day – had Katy and Rihanna fallen out? Did Rihanna disapprove of who Katy was marrying? (After all, this was a man who had posted a photo of himself in a wedding dress on Twitter, with one finger in the air!) Katy was quick to rise to her pal's defence a few weeks after the big day. 'I was upset she couldn't make it, but let me promise you, there was no one more upset about it than her,' Katy told *Now* magazine. 'When you have an album coming out you don't have a spare second in the day and you're answerable to the record company. She felt really bad she couldn't be there but we're still the very best of friends. My girl organised the best bachelorette party ever and I'll always love her to bits. It was just one of those really unfortunate things.'

In fact, the pair soon showed how close they were – recording a track together that they will release in the future. 'We're actually working on some music together – hell, yeah,' Rihanna told MTV. 'I would love to tour with Katy, she's a rock star. And when I see her live, she just brings such a fun vibe, like a colourful rock star. She has all these props. She has candy and fruit and a blown-up chap-stick on stage, but then she's rocking out with a guitar and banging her head and swinging on stage and crowd-surfing. That's the s*** that just makes you excited when you see her perform. She's beautiful, but then she rocks out.'

Katy returned the compliment in an interview with *Grazia* magazine. 'What I like about her [Rihanna] is she doesn't get all wrapped up. There's no attitude. Some people get famous and too big for their britches. They live in their world with no room for anyone else. I'm not like that and nor is she.'

Rumour has it that a hen night wasn't the only thing Rihanna gave her pal Katy in the run-up to her wedding, either – feeling awful that she couldn't make the ceremony, Rihanna reportedly gave the newlyweds a second honeymoon, too. According to the *Sun*, a source close to Rihanna told them: 'Rihanna hasn't stopped apologising . . . she told Katy she'd been racking her brains about how to make it up to them. She knows how much Katy loves Tokyo, so she gave them a trip they could always remember.' The holiday – which the *Sun* reported cost £30,000 – included four nights at the Dynasty suite (at a cost of £1,500 a night) at the Mandarin Oriental hotel in Tokyo, and first-class flights. Boasting stunning views of Tokyo City with Mount Fuji in the background, the suite is stunning, with three rooms packed with fine art, LCD televisions in each room, and a marble bathroom. It was certainly a generous gift.

Finally, the wedding day of 23 October was upon the excited bride and groom. Despite press speculation, the couple stressed that they wanted a 'normal' wedding, with Russell telling the US TV show *The View*: 'We just love each other and we want to get married in front of our friends and family and keep it very normal. It will have a first dance, it will have all of those things, like anything else,' he added. 'It's no more interesting or no less spectacular than any marriage of anybody, so it's very beautiful and incredible and wonderful, but it's also utterly mundane.'

Well, not everyone would call a six-day party with a wedding in the middle 'mundane'! The pair did keep the wedding reasonably small, however, with just eighty guests arriving in India for the ceremony. The night before the wedding, there was an engagement ceremony for them all to enjoy, with Katy wearing a maroon sari while she partied to Bollywood tunes with Russell, clad in a kurta (traditional collarless Hindi) pyjama.

Then, on the Saturday, all the guests were treated to a wedding unlike any they had seen before. With the outside of the resort hidden from prying cameras by bamboo screens, the venue itself was decorated with pretty lamps and flower garlands, creating a stunning setting for the romantic evening. Snake charmers, fire jugglers and dancers entertained the guests, while Russell made his entrance on a horse, flanked by camels and elephants, before walking around a fire with his fiancée, chanting traditional mantras. He had also arranged a surprise for his new bride – the gift of a Bengal tiger named Machli as a token of his love – while Katy surprised him with a present of her own, a baby elephant (both animals will remain at the Ranthambore National Park, where Russell is paying a gamekeeper to take care of them).

The ceremony was performed by a friend of Katy's family, a Christian minister in keeping with the beliefs she grew up with. At 5 p.m., local time, Russell and Katy sat on wedding thrones while exchanging their vows. Katy looked stunning in a dove-grey, lace Elie Saab dress – one of three gowns she dressed in for the festivities (the others she wore later were designed by Zuhair Murad and Donna Mizani). Throughout the moving ceremony, traditional music was played and Rajasthani folk musicians sang. Following the wedding, the guests found thirteen vehicles waiting, ready to whisk them all off on a safari!

The couple, who had finally managed to keep the press at bay – for the ceremony at least – issued a statement following their magical wedding. 'Katy and Russell are overjoyed to confirm that they were pronounced Mr and Mrs Brand on Saturday, October 23. The very private and spiritual ceremony, attended by the couple's closest family and friends, was performed by a Christian minister and long-time friend of the Hudson family. The backdrop was the inspirational and majestic countryside of Northern India.'

Katy later explained to *Grazia* magazine: 'We never wanted it to be a public event, which is why we didn't sell pictures, so we had some privacy. This relationship is real. It's not a photo opportunity, it's two people who have found what they want.'

With festivities continuing over the rest of the weekend, Russell and Katy snuck quietly away on the morning of Monday, 25 October, Katy's twenty-sixth birthday. Boarding a helicopter to Jaipur, the newlyweds then flew to the Maldives . . . just as more trouble came their way.

On the same day, Rajasthan state's chief minister ordered an investigation into public complaints of noise from the wedding festivities. Excessive noise is banned after 10 p.m.

as it disturbs locals and the wildlife, and five days into Katy and Russell's honeymoon, they heard the news that they had been dreading – the managers at the Aman-i-Khás hotel were being charged with violating noise laws. Sawai Madhopur district official Ravi Kumar Surpur announced that the couple would not be charged, but the hotel staff could face a fine or possible jail time for exceeding the forty-five-decibel noise limit allowed in the area.

And to top it off, newspapers reported that, while on honeymoon in the Maldives at the Soneva Fushi resort, things may not have been going that well. While staying at the beautiful hotel, which boasts villas with their own pools and even a tree-house to stay in, tabloids reported that Katy had been bitten by a spider that left her needing medication for a rash on her leg. Happily, Katy was quick to set the record straight. 'I've not been bitten by a spider. I'll file this 1 in the ever growing cabinet of false information that has been at its PEAK as of late . . . ' she wrote on Twitter.

Although their wedding had been beautiful, and they had managed to keep away from the prying eyes of the paparazzi, it seemed that even their most private day had become a tabloid frenzy . . .

11

Mrs Russell Brand

K aty and Russell had managed what many celebrity couples have failed to do when they kept their wedding private and personal. While stories of elephants, traditional dancing and exotic gifts at the ceremony circulated in the press, no one really knew many details of the marriage itself, or of the couple's romantic Maldives honeymoon. It was a brief, private break for the pair and a much-needed rest for both of them. While Katy had been writing, recording and promoting her album *Teenage Dream*, Russell had spent much of late 2009 and 2010 working on two movies – a new film version of Shakespeare's *The Tempest*, and a remake of the Dudley Moore comedy *Arthur* – as well as providing a voice for a third, the animated comedy *Despicable Me*.

Filmed in beautiful Hawaii, *The Tempest* starred Helen Mirren as Prospera, the Duchess of Milan (director Julie Taymor decided to take the male lead part of Prospero and make it female). When she is usurped by her brother, she is cast off with her young daughter Miranda on a raft and left to die, but they survive and find themselves on an island inhabited by the mysterious Caliban. There, Prospera intends to use magic she has learnt to exact her revenge on those who have wronged her. Russell got to play the role of the clown Trinculo, one of the more light-hearted characters in the production. It would be the first time he worked with Helen Mirren, but they were to re-team a few months later for Russell's second leading role in a movie (the first being in *Get Him to the Greek*).

Russell had been cast in the title role for the movie *Arthur*, set to be released in the spring of 2011. A remake of the 1981 film starring Dudley Moore and Liza Minnelli, it's the story of a man with a seemingly limitless fortune who spends most of his time drinking and playing around like a child. Only his nanny, Hobson (Helen Mirren), is able to keep him out of trouble, but things are about to get sticky when he falls in love with a girl his family doesn't approve of, and risks his fortune in the process. Filmed in New York with a cast that includes Nick Nolte and Jennifer Garner, the movie was directed by Jason Winer, best known for his work on the hit US TV comedy *Modern Family*.

While Russell was resting from such a busy schedule, for Katy the honeymoon was just a temporary respite before even more work began. First, shortly after the wedding, she announced that she would spend much of 2011 on tour. Her tour was named the California Dreams tour and would begin in February 2011 with dates in Lisbon, Milan, Zurich, Munich, Berlin and Paris before arriving in London in mid-March, followed by Manchester, Liverpool, Dublin and Glasgow. During April and May, Katy would take the live show to Australia and New Zealand, followed by Japan. Then the tour would return to the UK for even more dates in October.

She also had another single to promote. Her third release from the *Teenage Dreams* album was to be the extremely catchy song 'Firework', one of Katy's favourites. 'People are coming back [to that song] and almost adopting it as their own anthem, and it's hard, I think, to write an anthem that's not cheesy,' she told *MTV News*. 'And I hope that this could be something in that category. I hope this could be one of those things where it's like, "Yeah, I want to put my fist up and feel proud and feel strong." But I also don't want to be cheesy. It's a fine line, and I think "Firework" . . . would be, like, the opus or my one song – if I had to pick a song to play – 'cause it has a great beat. But it also has a fantastic message.'

She told the *Daily Mail*: 'I think that in life, people are challenged to get to where they want to be and to reach their goals. Hopefully they can hear this song and find out that those challenges aren't really difficult to get past.'

Written by Katy with Stargate (a production/songwriting team who have also worked with Beyoncé and Rihanna), Sandy Vee (who has worked with the Black Eyed Peas) and Ester Dean (who has written songs for Mary J. Blige, Ciara, Rihanna and Christina Aguilera), the song is about being strong and showing everyone just who you are: 'Do you know that there's still a chance for you / 'Cause there's a spark in you / You just gotta ignite, the light, and let it shine / Just own the night like the fourth of July / 'Cause baby you're a firework / Come on, show 'em what you're worth / Make 'em go "Oh, oh, oh" / As you shoot across the sky . . . '

Her new husband had been something of an inspiration for this song, too. Russell showed Katy a passage from one of his favourite books, Jack Kerouac's *On the Road*, that he thought described Katy. 'It was a paragraph that he said I was like,' she told the BBC's *Newsbeat*. 'In the book he was talking about how he wanted to be around people who were buzzing, fizzing and making people go "Argh, like fireworks across the sky". I guess that's my whole vibe. I want to make people go "Argh" in so many different ways. I want to be a living firework.'

With a striking photo for the single's cover, featuring a bare-shouldered Katy with spiky hair, shot by celebrity photographer Rankin, Katy needed a memorable video to match. But how could she top the 'California Gurls' video, in which she wore a cupcake bra and fired whipped cream from it? Simple. In this video, she would shoot fireworks from her chest instead.

Katy wanted the video to be something extra special, so she called for 250 extras, who should all be real-life inspirational people 'that are buzzing and fizzing and have the potential to become fireworks', to appear in her video. She explained on her website what she was looking for. 'With my story, it's been so many trials and tribulations to get to this place. It's amazing to hear people get through things in life and reach their goals,' she wrote. 'Music can be so powerful and I think it can transform you and inspire you and heal you. We're basically making a formation of a firework, all the kids are being the sparks around me. The whole vibe of the video shoot is a movement, an emotional experience.'

The video begins with Katy singing on a rooftop in Budapest. We see unhappy children – a brother and sister covering their ears while their parents row, a bald cancer patient sitting alone in a hospital room, a young man alone at a club, a shy girl in heavy clothes sitting on the edge of a pool not joining in with her friends in bikinis – and as the chorus begins, fireworks shoot from Katy across the sky. The shy girl begins taking off her clothes, the cancer patient walks from the hospital, the children run from their parents, the young man crosses the dancefloor to kiss another man as fireworks shoot from them all. As fireworks fill the sky, hundreds of kids join Katy on the streets to dance.

It was the first pop music video to feature so many fans in one location, and with the help of Deutsche Telekom Katy made an accompanying documentary short film that followed some of the kids from their homes to the location in Budapest. Eight countries in Europe had run the competition to appear in the video using online contests in Germany, Austria, Hungary, the Czech Republic, Slovakia, Poland, Macedonia and Montenegro, and more than 38,000 entries were received. 'It's been a fantastic partnership with Deutsche Telekom and it's been a great way to include people that are interested in me, my music and my music video,' Katy said of the project.

It's a striking video, as directed by award-winning director Dave Meyers, who has worked with Pink, Missy Elliott, Dido and Kelly Clarkson. Katy dedicated it to the It Gets Better Project (www.itgetsbetter.org), an organisation that encourages kids to fight back against discrimination. Their pledge is thus: 'Everyone deserves to be respected for who they are. I pledge to spread this message to my friends, family and neighbours. I'll speak up against hate and intolerance whenever I see it, at school and at work. I'll provide hope for lesbian, gay, bi, trans and other bullied teens by letting them know that It Gets Better.'

Katy tweeted her support. 'I am officially dedicating my new video to It Gets Better because everyone has the spark to be a FIREWORK.'

While the song was released on 26 October 2010 – the day Katy and Russell headed off to the Maldives for their honeymoon, and the day after her twenty-sixth birthday – she was soon back to promote the single. First stop was the MTV Europe Music Awards, which was being held in Madrid on 7 November. The ceremony was taking place at the Caja Mágica (meaning 'the magic box'), the sports stadium where the Madrid Masters tennis tournament is held each year.

The presenter of the ceremony was to be Eva Longoria, one of the stars of *Desperate Housewives*, and performers included Rihanna, Miley Cyrus, Bon Jovi and Kings of Leon. Katy performed 'Firework' on an outside stage wearing a very Freddie Mercury-esque white unitard emblazoned with a big crystal red flame as fireworks exploded around her. She was also nominated for five awards – as was her chart rival, Lady Gaga. Katy was up for Best Song, Best Video (both for 'California Gurls'), Best Female, Best Pop Act, and Best World Stage Performance. While Lady Gaga won three awards, Katy only got to take home the award for Best Video. The winner was announced by British model Kelly Brook, and Katy left her seat beside Russell and made her way down to the stage in a tiny dress and very high heels. 'Thank you so much, this is awesome!' she told her cheering fans. 'I really want to thank you guys because I was just on stage performing to you and you were the best f***ing crowd in Europe.

I really want to say thank you so much to everybody that helped me make this music video and song, Snoop Dogg!'

Katy had little time to enjoy winning her new award, as she had to fly to New York to appear at the Victoria's Secret Fashion Show on 11 November. An annual fashion show presented by the lingerie brand Victoria's Secret, the event began in 1995 and has been televised since 2001. It is well known for its use of famous models wearing extravagant and elaborate underwear, and for the star musical perform-ances that pepper the show.

Over the years, the show has had some memorable moments, from Tyra Banks announcing that she was retir-ing and that her appearance at the 2005 show was her last as a professional model, to the first US performance from the re-formed Spice Girls in 2007.

While it is hugely popular, the show has also had its fair share of criticism for being a feature-length commercial for the Victoria's Secret brand, and even for being 'pornograph-ic', for featuring women modelling underwear. According to one report, the Federal Communications Commission in the USA receives hundreds of complaints every year when the show is broadcast, including some from the National Organisation of Women, who have described it as 'a soft-core porn infomercial'. Along with the Concerned Women of America and Parents Television Council groups, they wrote to CBS (who broadcast the show in the USA) in 2002 ask-ing them not to broadcast it at all. 'What purpose does the special serve except to overly sexualize women and use this to bolster the networks' demographics for young men?' they asked in a letter to the president of the TV network. CBS, meanwhile, responded by saying: 'This is not pornography. It's a one-hour fashion show mixed with musical perform-ances and comedy segments.' CBS spokesman Chris Ender continued: 'Does it push the envelope? Sure. But everyone knows what the Victoria's Secret fashion show is. With the advance publicity and the content advisory, every viewer will be armed with information to make their own choice.'

Each year, the show is a huge hit, watched by millions; to add to the excitement, every year a jewellery designer is asked to make a 'fantasy bra' to be worn by one of the mod-els in the show. The one created in 2000 and worn by Gisele Bündchen has appeared in the *Guinness Book of Records* as being the most expensive piece of lingerie ever made, valued at $15 million. It was made of red satin and covered in more than 1,300 gems, including 300 carats of Thai rubies sur-rounded by diamonds. For 2010, the bra was slightly more affordable – designed by Damiani and modelled by Adriana Lima, the Bombshell Fantasy bra was a snip at $2 million.

Katy Perry and R&B artist Akon were both asked to per-form at the show in 2010. Katy performed 'Firework', appear-ing on the runway in a lilac-coloured corset with a train and pink crystal and feather hairpiece. The train was pulled away to reveal a puff-ball-style skirt with a firework design. She also performed a medley of her hits 'Teenage Dream', 'California Gurls' and 'Hot n Cold' in a cartoony dress and lace-up knee boots while some of the models strutted the catwalk.

Then, following the after-show party, Katy was off to London to launch her next project. It wasn't a single, album or video – it was a perfume. Presented in a purple, cat-shaped bottle (complete with crystals for eyes), Purr was launched in Selfridges with Katy on hand in a stunning purple dress to announce its arrival. Thousands of fans gathered at the store on Oxford Street, London, to see Katy, who spent hours greeting them as well as giving away 100 signed perfume boxes for the first customers. 'I'm really happy to present Purr here in London first,' she told reporters at the event. 'Next week it will be New York City. It'll be fantastic. And I'm so happy it's in Selfridges, it has a very classy air around it. Thank you for coming out,' she told the gathered fans and press, 'I'm really excited to be able to meet some of you guys and sign your bottles, your whiskers, paws . . . whatever you need to be signed!'

Katy had made no secret of the fact that she wanted her own fragrance, just like stars Britney Spears and Beyoncé. 'There is a wonderful world of fragrances out there, but like with my music, I believe there is room for me and my own unique twist on it.'

She certainly had fun with the presentation. As well as the cat-shaped bottle, Katy posed on the fragrance's website dressed in a pink and purple latex catsuit, complete with tail, next to a huge ball of pink yarn. A fan of cats – she has made a star of her own pet, Kitty Purry, by regularly mentioning the puss on her blog – Katy wanted the perfume to be cute and sexy. 'I'm absolutely thrilled to finally introduce me in a bottle!' she wrote on the katyperrybeauty.co.uk website. 'Purr is a natural extension of who I am as a woman. It's a gorgeous blend of all my favourite scents and embodies my style, my tastes and my love for all things incredibly cute. It is an absolutely purrfect perfume that I hope leaves you meowing with delight!'

Featuring top notes of peach nectar, green bamboo and apple, the fragrance includes floral scents such as white jasmine, freesia and rose, mixed with vanilla orchid, white amber and sandalwood. It was an instant hit, and Katy followed up her launch in Selfridges with another in New York just days later, driving around the city in a van, stopping to meet and greet fans.

There was no time for pausing to enjoy her latest success, however, as she then hopped on a plane to attend the American Music Awards in Los Angeles. Unlike other award ceremonies that are voted for by Katy's music peers, the AMAs are voted for by the music-buying public, with the original list of nominations based on airplay, sales and video viewing figures. Michael Jackson remains the most celebrated artist at the AMAs, having won twenty-six awards during his career, while Whitney Houston is the most celebrated female in the show's history, having won a total of twenty-two awards.

The 2010 awards were held on 21 November at the Nokia Theater in Los Angeles. Christina Aguilera, Rihanna, Bon Jovi, the Black Eyed Peas and Pink were among the performers at the ceremony, and Katy sang 'Firework' accompanied by a children's choir (dressed in black with red sparkly bow ties). She was lowered onto the stage in a giant star, wearing a beautiful red gown that was ripped away to reveal she was wearing another Queen-style unitard. She was also nominated for three awards for Artist of the Year and Album of the Year (losing both to kiddie sensation Justin Bieber), and Favourite Female Artist (she lost to Lady Gaga), but could console herself with the thought that her performance was the most memorable of the night.

Also, just over a week later, Katy received some very good news. On 1 December, the nominations for the fifty-third Grammy Awards were announced. Eminem received ten nominations, Lady Gaga received six, and Katy received four nominations, along with her pal Rihanna, while Beyoncé and Alicia Keys each received two. Katy was in impressive company, and it was also announced that some legends would be in attendance at the awards on 13 February 2011 at the Staples Center in Los Angeles – Barbra Streisand would be presented with the MusiCares Person of the Year award, while Julie Andrews was among those receiving a Lifetime Achievement award.

Katy had been nominated for Album of the Year, Best Female Vocal (for 'Teenage Dream'), Best Pop Collaboration (for 'California Gurls', with Snoop Dogg) and Best Pop Vocal Album, and she was thrilled. Mentioning the nominations on Twitter, she wrote: 'It's an AMAZING honour to be nominated & recognized by my other hard working peers tonight. So happy that I trusted my gut w/ this record & thank u to all the AMAZING #TEAMKATY people I've been blessed to surround myself with . . . couldn't do it w/out u. It takes a village!'

More excitement was to come. While her debut on *Sesame Street* had been cut back in September due to her raunchy attire (Katy's cleavage obviously scared TV makers as her 34D chest was also reduced in a poster promoting her appearance on VH1 in November), Katy had been asked to appear on another landmark show, *The Simpsons*.

The Simpsons is, of course, the longest-running animated series of all time. First broadcast as shorts during comedienne Tracey Ullman's sketch show in 1987, the yellow animated family got their own half-hour series in 1989. As almost everyone knows, the series focuses on the working-class family the Simpsons, led by lazy, balding dad Homer, blue beehive-haired mum Marge, and their kids, little rascal Bart, his brainy sister Lisa, and baby of the family Maggie. Set in the fictional town of Springfield (although there are a few towns called Springfield in the USA, creator Matt Groening refuses to say if it is meant to be any of them), the series also features numerous oddball residents including nuclear plant owner Mr Burns and his grovelling assistant Smithers, bar owner Moe, school principal Skinner and Homer's annoying, cheery neighbour Ned Flanders. The ground-breaking show, which reached its twenty-second season at the end of 2010, has run to more than 470 episodes. Since 1989 it has won twenty-seven Emmy awards, while on 31 December 1999 *Time* magazine named *The Simpsons* the twentieth century's best television series and it was also awarded its own star on the Hollywood Walk of Fame.

The Simpsons is famous for its use of guest actors. While some famous names have provided voices for recurring roles – *Frasier*'s Kelsey Grammer and David Hyde Pierce as serial-killer Sideshow Bob and his brother Cecil, for example – others have supplied their voices for just one episode. These appearances have won *The Simpsons* a place in the *Guinness Book of Records* for the Most Guest Stars Featured in a TV Series, and the list of guests who have lent their voices to characters reads like a who's who of major celebrities. Singer Tony Bennett, CNN presenter Larry King, Ringo Starr, Sting, Tom Jones, James Brown and Paul McCartney have all appeared as animated versions of themselves in the series, while the list of celebrities who have provided voices for fictional characters include Danny DeVito (as Homer's long-lost brother), Dustin Hoffman (as Lisa's substitute teacher), Elizabeth Taylor (as the voice of Maggie), Michelle Pfeiffer (as Mindy, who falls in love with Homer), and Kiefer Sutherland (as his *24* character Jack Bauer).

Katy was joining an illustrious list, and she was also asked to take part in an extra episode – the Christmas special, to be broadcast in America on 5 December. She was to appear as herself in a unique section of the episode, a special live-action segment in which Homer, Bart and family would appear as puppets alongside Katy. Referring to her *Sesame Street* debacle, *Simpsons* executive producer Al Jean announced her appearance by saying: 'In the wake of Elmo's terrible betrayal, the *Simpsons* puppets wish to announce they stand shoulder-to-shoulder with Katy Perry.'

The episode was entitled *The Fight Before Christmas*, and Katy had the honour of playing barman Moe's girlfriend, kissing Mr Burns (to which he replies 'I kissed a girl . . . and I liked it!'), and leading the gang in a rendition of a song called 'The 39 Days of Christmas'. Wearing a red PVC dress decorated with *Simpsons* characters, Katy's performance finishes during the end credits, when puppet Moe cheekily jumps up and tries to kiss her on the lips. When he fails, he says 'I'll just kiss your belly button', before putting his face near her crotch. Katy replies, 'That's not my belly button', and when Moe pulls away she cheekily says, 'But I didn't say stop!'

Christmas was now just around the corner, but Katy's schedule was still packed as 2010 neared its close. After her appearance on the family-friendly *Simpsons*, Katy did something a little more adult – appearing on the cover of US men's magazine *Maxim* in a lace-and-leather body corset and thigh-high boots. Katy had already been crowned number one in the magazine's annual 'Hot 100 sexiest women' list earlier in the year, beating such names as Angelina Jolie, *Avatar*'s Zoe Saldana and *Gossip Girl*'s Blake Lively, and she ended the year by posing provocatively for the magazine and being interviewed about being their number-one gal. 'It's a worldwide thing – the rest of the world makes it their standard,' she said. 'It's one of the questions they ask me in all interviews now, even in places where *Maxim* doesn't exist. I'll go to Timbuktu, and they'll be like, "You're the number-one hottest", and I'm like, "*Maxim* said so, but thank you so much for saying so in Timbuktu."'

She also mentioned her new husband in the interview, when asked about who her current celebrity crush was. 'I've said Justin Bieber [was my celebrity crush] quite a few times, but I think I'm over it now. I think it's probably safe to say I married my celebrity crush,' she told the magazine.

In fact, as 2010 drew to a close and Katy gave a series of interviews to the press, it seemed that hubby Russell was never far from her mind. She told *Grazia* magazine's Christmas issue how they were going to spend Christmas that year. 'There will be me and Russ and a pink Christmas tree and a tofu-urky. We'll open one present the night before because that's the tradition in my family,' she told the magazine. 'And we'll do something new. We'll start our own new tradition because we are a family now.'

The couple was clearly happy together. 'He's brilliant.

Every day he amazes me. He makes me laugh like no one else. We are each other's perfect match,' she added. 'If you really want to know what made me fall in love with him it was seeing how amazing he was with people, particularly with children. Russell has changed his life and wants to help other people change theirs. For all his naughtiness on the surface, underneath he's truly good. My parents adore him.'

It seemed that Katy was getting on with her in-law, too, as she revealed in an interview with *Now* magazine. Since marrying Russell in October, Katy had become close friends with his mum, Barbara, whom she greatly admires. 'Barbara has seen Russell in his darkest days, so she knows better than anyone how much he's changed. He's a devoted husband but if he steps out of line she and I are really close so she might even take my side!'

Russell confirmed the friendly relationship between his mum and new wife that started the moment they first met. 'Katy was lovely when she met my mum. She came round my mum's house. She's dead nice and normal, a down-to-earth easy-going sort of person. She's really, really sweet and easy to be around and she was lovely with my mum, they get on well. But you don't want them getting too much of an alliance going though, do you?!'

Katy did admit to TV presenter Ellen DeGeneres that she was quite a traditional girl in her marriage to Russell, even intending to take his name. 'Sometimes when people try to get my attention, like at an event or something, and they want special attention, they call me Mrs Brand,' she said, admitting that she really likes it.

So would a family be the next thing on the agenda for

Mr and Mrs Brand? Katy wouldn't be drawn, only admitting that Russell 'wants eleven boys, named after the West Ham team' sometime in the future. After all of Katy and Russell's eventful times throughout 2010, such an announcement from them actually wouldn't be that surprising . . .

12

The Future . . .

So what is next for Katy Perry Brand? At the age of just twenty-six, she can already boast that she has sold over thirty million singles worldwide, hosted the MTV Europe Music Awards, won Brit, MTV, People's Choice and *Glamour* magazine awards, launched her own perfume and made millions as her songs have become part of popular culture ('Hot n Cold', for example, has appeared on numerous TV and movie soundtracks including *The Ugly Truth*, *The Proposal*, and, best of all, *Alvin and the Chipmunks: The Squeakquel*).

It seems that she has already achieved many of the things it took one of her idols, Madonna, at least another ten years to do – Katy can proudly call herself a queen of pop and dance, a woman with her own sense of style whose music videos are just as memorable as 'Like a Prayer', 'Vogue' or 'Express Yourself' were more than two decades ago. There is, however, one area of the media that Madonna attempted (sometimes successfully, sometimes not) that Katy hasn't conquered . . . yet. Movies.

Early in her pop career, Madonna appeared – in a role strikingly similar to her own character at the time – as Susan in the hit comedy *Desperately Seeking Susan*. Winning praise from critics ('Madonna has never found a better fit than the role of Susan,' said *Time Out*), and boasting a smash-hit song on the soundtrack ('Into the Groove'), the movie propelled Madonna from singer to megastar in 1985. Her next few films weren't as successful – *Shanghai Surprise* and *Who's That Girl* bombed at the box office, and won her Razzie awards for Worst Actress of the Year, but then in 1990, Madonna won the role of sultry singer Breathless Mahoney in Warren Beatty's *Dick Tracy*. The memorable performance included her singing 'Sooner or Later', written by acclaimed songwriter Stephen Sondheim, a song Madonna performed at the Oscars (where it also won Best Original Song).

Next, came further acclaim for her performance in *A League of Their Own*, with Tom Hanks and Geena Davis. Then, in 1996, Madonna got the role she had always wanted, as Eva Perón in the musical *Evita*. Again, she was praised for her performance, and while she hasn't matched it since (her only acting roles in the last few years have been in the dire rom-com *The Next Best Thing* and in a small part as a Bond baddie in *Die Another Day*, a film for which she supplied the theme song), she has stayed connected to the movie business, now as a director for the movie *W. E.*, about the controversial romance between King Edward VIII and Mrs Wallis Simpson.

So will Katy's next move be to follow Madonna onto the big screen? She has already dipped her toe in the waters of Hollywood, appearing in the comedy *Get Him to the Greek*, starring future husband Russell Brand, although her performance was cut from the final film. Now Katy has finally picked up a leading role in the movies . . . sort of.

While she isn't actually seen on our cinema screens, Katy's voice takes centre-stage in one of the most fun movies of 2011. It isn't a superhero film or a sequel, and it isn't based on the latest hit teenage novel. It's a movie about a group of characters whose figurines we used to get free with BP petrol in the late 1970s. Yes, the Smurfs are back! And Katy Perry *is* the voice of Smurfette!

In case the cute little blue creatures have passed you by, here's a quick catch-up on the world of the Smurfs. Created back in 1958 as characters in a comic strip by Belgian cartoonist Peyo, the Smurfs are little blue people who all look very similar – blue skin, white trousers, white hat – and most of them are supposed to be around 100 years old. It was, in fact, Peyo's wife, Nine Culliford, who chose the colour, as she told *Time* magazine. 'They couldn't be green – they would have vanished into the vegetation. Red would have been too flashy, and yellow a bit unfortunate. Only blue was left!'

Among the characters are Handy Smurf (he wears white overalls instead of trousers and keeps a pencil behind his ear), Brainy Smurf (wearing large specs), Hefty Smurf (gasp, he has a tattoo!), Dreamy Smurf and Clumsy Smurf, while Papa Smurf (who has a beard and gets to wear red instead of white clothes) is the wise older one in charge and babe Smurfette one of the few female Smurfs.

The happy little fellows (and gals) eat smurfberries, live in toadstool-like houses in the middle of a forest and have an enemy – the evil sorcerer Gargamel (who actually created Smurfette himself . . . hmmm . . .) and his cat Azrael. Gargamel usually wants to either capture the Smurfs and eat them, or use them in a potion to make gold.

While the Smurfs have remained popular in much of Europe for fifty years (in Peyo's native Belgium there was a fiftieth-anniversary five-Euro coin made in 2008), their heyday in the UK was during the 1980s when they featured in a series of adverts for BP, and kids were able to collect little plastic versions of the Smurfs whenever their parents bought a few gallons of petrol at a BP garage. There was also Smurf pasta, a Smurf cereal and Smurf sweets (magic stars), all tying in nicely with an animated series that was shown on Saturday mornings in the USA and UK from 1981 to 1989.

It's this series that is probably the one you'll remember when you think of the word Smurf. Made by Hanna-Barbera, the animation company responsible for *The Flintstones*, *Scooby-Doo, Where Are You!* and *Top Cat*, the show ran for an impressive 256 episodes over a decade and won a Daytime Emmy award for Outstanding Children's Entertainment Series in 1983. As well as being a fun show about the travails of these little blue cuties, *The Smurfs* was educational, too – each episode had a moral and was backed by classical music such as Elgar's 'Pomp and Circumstance', Mendelssohn's 'Spring Song' and Mozart's *The Magic Flute*.

Throughout the 1980s, toyshop shelves boasted tons of Smurf merchandise and the figurines became very collectable (over 300 million have been made to date). There was also the teeth-grindingly catchy tune 'The Smurf Song' by Dutch singer Father Abraham, that went to number one in the charts in 1977 in sixteen countries, and a series of albums released by the Smurfs, as well as a Barron Knights parody single that became a bestseller in the UK.

It's no wonder that Hollywood saw the potential to make

a feature-length movie about the blue characters, although it has been a long time in the making. There was a simple animated movie, *The Smurfs and the Magic Flute*, in 1976, that was released worldwide in 1983, and a few feature-length TV movies in the Eighties. Since 2003, however, a big-budget Smurf movie has been in the pipeline, and finally in 2010 it went into production. From the moment the film was announced, the press speculated about who would play the Smurfs. At one point, Quentin Tarantino (a Smurf fan) was tipped to be the voice of Brainy Smurf. 'There were conversations about it, but it didn't work out,' said Hannah Minghella, president of Sony Pictures Animation, who were making the movie. Instead, *Saturday Night Live*'s Fred Armisen took the part, while comic actor Jonathan Winters signed on as Papa Smurf, George Lopez as Grouchy Smurf, *Hitch* star Kevin James as Hefty Smurf, British actor Alan Cumming as Gutsy Smurf and, of course, Katy Perry as Smurfette. Hank Azaria, best known for the voices he provides in *The Simpsons*, is bad-guy Gargamel, while the two main live-action roles are played by *How I Met Your Mother*'s Neil Patrick Harris and *Glee*'s Jayma Mays, as a couple who meet the blue creatures when the Smurfs leave their happy homes and end up in the real world.

'We liked the idea of juxtaposing the Smurf values with the modern world,' Minghella explained to *Time* magazine. 'Smurfs grow their own food and are very environmentally conscious. They don't have technology or electricity. They do everything together and are really supportive of each other. For us, that was the starting point. Let's bring that magic into the real world.'

With Katy Perry playing the sexy Smurfette, she has

once again caused controversy in her parents' household. 'I'd never seen an episode because my parents wouldn't let me! My mother thought that Smurfette was a little bit slutty, being the only female in the village. And now I've shown her,' Katy jokes. 'I called her up and said, "Guess what, ma? I'm Smurfette!"'

Katy figures it is the perfect part for her: 'I always feel like a cartoon on a pretty frequent basis, when I'm dressing up, and especially on stage, so I think it was just natural. After all, I am Smurfalicious!'

It's sure to be the first acting role of many for Katy – if she can find the time. She kicked off 2011 with the sell-out California Dreams world tour after spending the last few months of 2010 winning awards, making TV appearances and giving live performances to promote the album *Teenage Dream*.

There have also been lots of rumours as to what the future holds. Now happily married to Russell Brand, could a family be the next project on the horizon? When Russell's *Booky Wook 2: This Time It's Personal* was published in September 2010, she tweeted that his next book should probably be titled *The Double Ds: Dishes and Diapers*, sending the press into a frenzy of speculation for the second time in a year that a little Perry Brand could be on the way.

And if the Brands aren't planning a family, newspaper gossip columnists speculate that Katy could become one of the judges on Simon Cowell's US version of *The X Factor*, following her guest appearances on the British original in 2010. Although Cheryl Cole is also tipped for the role, it looks as though Katy, with her wit and cheeky outspokenness, is the likely candidate to become one of the most famous faces on American TV. 'I saw something about that [becoming an *X-Factor* judge] and I think Simon is flirting with me through the press,' Katy told *Cosmopolitan* magazine in November 2010. 'He is a big flirt. I know a lot of it is rumour. But sometimes rumours turn into reality!'

Whatever Katy chooses to do, it looks like she and her new husband will be very busy during the second decade of the twenty-first century. Russell's film, TV and comedy career mean that he regularly needs to be on both sides of the Atlantic, whether he is performing live or promoting his latest movie, *Arthur* (a remake of the 1981 Dudley Moore movie, in which Brand plays a drunken playboy who falls for a woman his family doesn't like). And Katy will be adding to those frequent-flier miles, too, with her tour and the promotional work she'll need to do for *The Smurfs*, so it looks as if – for the foreseeable future, at least – the happy couple will be dividing their time between their homes in Los Angeles, London and New York.

However, in an interview with the *Sun*, Katy hinted that in the not-so-distant future, she would like to really settle down . . . in the English countryside. 'I want to do something quintessentially British like buy a big farmhouse and have our children running around in the fresh air,' she says. 'I would want to do it properly, though. I would expect Russell to be up milking cows and collecting eggs from the chickens while I run the farm shop and bake pies.'

'It might sound like I am kidding,' she continues, 'but once Russell has made all the movies he wants and after I have made all the music I want, it would be the perfect place to start a family. England is still so green in parts, and it's where I would like us to raise a family.'

She even joked to *Grazia* magazine that she would like to become more than just the wife of a Brit. 'I want a British passport. Actually, I want a title, I want to be Lady Katy Brand – I've told him that I would like for him to be knighted . . . you never know with us Brands!'

Katy Perry – could she be our next Nigella Lawson? Or Lady of the Manor? All we can do is wait and see what this fun, refreshing, beautiful woman is going to choose to do next, and then go along for the ride. It promises to be a wild and crazy one . . .

Timeline

25 OCTOBER 1984

Katheryn Elizabeth Hudson is born to parents Mary (née Perry) and Keith in Santa Barbara, California. They already have a daughter, Angela Ann, who was born on 7 December 1982.

1987

Katy's brother David is born.

1988–1995

Katy and her family travel around the western USA with her pastor father, who preaches his beliefs to local communities.

1993

Katy sings for the first time at the Oasis Christian Center in Santa Barbara.

1995

Katy and her family stop travelling with the church and settle permanently in Santa Barbara.

SPRING 1997

Katy appears in the local production of *Fiddler on the Roof*, at the Santa Barbara High School Theater. She appears onstage as an extra, and meets her first boyfriend, Timo Nunez Belami, who is also in the production.

SUMMER 1997

Katy goes away to summer camp and ends her relationship with Timo by letter on 5 August.

25 OCTOBER 1997

Katy is given her first guitar for her thirteenth birthday, from the pastors at her church.

SEPTEMBER 1998

She starts attending Dos Pueblos High School in Goleta.

SEPTEMBER 1999

Katy takes her GED and passes, earning herself the equivalent of a high-school diploma. She drops out of school.

OCTOBER 1999

After being spotted by Nashville music producers, Katy is invited to record an album in Nashville, so spends the next few months travelling between the city and her Santa Barbara home.

2000

Katy signs to Red Hill Records and records tracks for her first Christian album. 'I started going to Nashville to record some gospel songs, and to be around amaz-ing country-music vets and learn how to craft a song and play guitar. I'd actually have to super-glue the tips of my fingers because they hurt so much from playing guitar all day, you know? And from that, I made the best record I could make as a gospel singer at fifteen.'

AUGUST 2001

Katy Hudson the album is released, including the tracks 'Trust in Me', written by Katy, 'When There's Nothing Left', 'My Own Monster' and the trance-y 'Faith Won't Fail'. Weeks later, Red Hill Records closes down and the CDs are thrown away. Katy returns home and starts to listen to different types of music, including Queen, the Beach Boys and No Doubt while she thinks about changing her musical style. ('I wanted to be like Freddie Mercury.')

LATE 2001

Katy sees a documentary about singer Alanis Morissette and learns she had worked with a producer/writer called Glen Ballard. She gets her manager to arrange a meeting with him. 'I had my dad drive me up to LA. I said, "Dad, stay in the car. I'm just gonna go in, play a song for this guy and come back out." And I did, and I guess it went well, because I got the call the next day.'

2002

Katy moves to Los Angeles, aged seventeen, and starts a two-year working relationship with Glen Ballard, writing tracks and recording them for an album. She is offered a record deal with Island Def Jam, but they ultimately decide not to release the album and she is dropped from the label.

SEPTEMBER 2004

Katy signs to her third record label, Columbia, and begins work with production team The Matrix (Lauren Christy, her husband Graham Edwards and Scott Spock), who had worked with Avril Lavinge (including hit 'Complicated'), Britney Spears ('Shadow'), Shakira ('Don't Bother') and boy-band Busted ('A Present for Everyone'). The album is shelved, however.

MAY 2005

One of Katy's songs, 'Simple', recorded with Glenn Ballard, appears on the soundtrack for *The Sisterhood of the Traveling Pants*.

2006

With no record deal, Katy gets a job working for Taxi Music ('I had to sit in a cubicle and listen to other people's songs all day. Most were horrible, and I just wanted to warn the singers about what they were getting into.')

When she isn't working, she records guest vocals on a song called 'Goodbye for Now' by the Christian rock-metal band P.O.D. ('Payable on Death') and she also appears in the video for Carbon Leaf's song 'Learn to Fly', as a girl trying to get to one of their gigs.

8 FEBRUARY 2006

Angelica Cob-Baehler of Katy's former label Columbia, tells Virgin Records talent-scout Chris Anokute about Katy at the forty-eighth Grammy Awards at Los Angeles' Staples Center. After hearing a demo of Katy's music, he convinces his boss, Jason Flom, to see Katy live on stage at a showcase at LA's Viper Room.

LATE 2006

Flom is won over and Katy is offered a record deal at Capitol/Virgin ('Jason Flom called me. That day I went out for coffee and never went back.'). She also begins a relationship with Gym Class Heroes singer Travis McCoy after appearing in the band's video for 'Cupid's Chokehold'.

EARLY 2007

Katy starts work on the tracks that will make up *One of the Boys*, her first album. She works with producers including Dr Luke and Greg Wells.

NOVEMBER 2007

Katy films a low-budget video for the song 'Ur So Gay' and it is released onto the internet. The song gets some buzz behind it and no lesser star than Madonna says it is her favourite song of the moment. The video features Katy, in a Fifties-style polka-dot dress, sitting on some fake grass with plastic daisies around her with animated clouds floating by. As she sings and plays her guitar, the video's story is played out by Ken- and Barbie-style dolls.

DECEMBER 2007

The single 'Ur So Gay' is sold with a 'Parental Advisory' sticker warning of sexual content/strong language.

JANUARY 2008

Entertainment Weekly magazine gives the song a rave review: 'I know the lyrics to Katy Perry's "Ur So Gay" are eighteen different kinds of wrong – the opening line about what she'd like her wayward beau to do with his H&M scarf is not for the faint of heart, nor is it entirely safe for work – but I can't stop playing this jaunty little ditty on repeat . . . Listen for yourself and tell me if you don't love it, too.'

10 MARCH 2008

Katy makes a guest appearance in an episode of the TV series *Wildfire*, appearing as herself in an episode entitled *Life's Too Short*.

6 MAY 2008

'I Kissed a Girl' is released as a single in the USA. There are mixed reactions to the song's racy lyrics – a church in Ohio posts a sign outside saying 'I kissed a girl and I liked it, then I went to Hell'. Meanwhile a website run by Focus on the Family (a US Christian group) reviews the single and claims that Katy is 'living down to a damaging, demeaning, "girls gone wild" stereotype'.

JUNE 2008

After rejecting a $300 ring and going for a more elaborate one, Travis presents Katy with flowers and a promise ring. On his own finger, he also starts wearing a silver band inscribed with Katy's name.

JUNE 2008

Singer-songwriter Jill Sobule, who, in 1995, recorded a song called 'I Kissed a Girl', rants about Katy on The Rumpus, a culture website, saying: 'F*** you, Katy Perry, you f***ing stupid, maybe "not good for the gays," title thieving, haven't heard much else, so not quite sure if you're talented, f***ing little slut.' She later reveals that the rant had been in jest and that she had meant no offence to Katy at all.

13 JUNE 2008

'I Kissed a Girl' is the number-one best-selling pop song on iTunes, and the most requested song on New York's influential Z100, and the video has over two million hits in its first two weeks on MySpace.

17 JUNE 2008

Katy's first album at Capitol, *One of the Boys*, is released in the USA.

20 JUNE 2008

Katy joins the Warped Tour, playing with over 100 different acts throughout the USA in cities such as San Francisco, Denver, Dallas, Miami, Montreal and Milwaukee until 17 August. She is joined on the tour by boyfriend Travis and his band Gym Class Heroes.

9 AUGUST 2008

Onstage in George, Washington, Katy pulls sixteen-year-old fan Jenna Buhmann onto the stage and kisses her while performing 'I Kissed a Girl'. 'She looked me right in the eyes for about fifteen seconds, and that's when I knew it was going to happen,' says Jenna. 'I puckered up my lips, she let go of the bodyguard's arm, grabbed my arm and pulled me towards her. I grabbed her face, put my hand on the back of her head and just kissed her. The crowd went crazy.'

18 AUGUST 2008

Katy's mother, Mary, is interviewed about Katy and lets the world know her feelings about 'I Kissed a Girl'. 'I hate the song,' she says. 'It clearly promotes homosexuality and its message is shameful and disgusting. Katy knows how I feel. We are a very out-spoken family. I can't even listen to that song. The first time I heard it I was in total shock. When it comes on the radio I bow my head and pray.'

SEPTEMBER 2008

Katy embarks on a mini-tour of Europe, and plays the

Scala in London with singer Adele.

2 SEPTEMBER 2008

British gay rights activist Peter Tatchell criticises Katy's songs, especially 'Ur So Gay', in the press. 'I am sure Katy would get a critical reception if she expressed comparable sentiments in a song called "Ur So Black, Jewish or Disabled".'

7 SEPTEMBER 2008

Katy appears at the MTV Video Music Awards in Los Angeles, where she is nominated in five categories: Best Female Video, Best New Artist, Best Art Direction, Best Editing and Best Cinematography for the video. Unfortunately, she does not win any prizes. The awards are hosted by Russell Brand, who asks Katy – along with singer Pink – to film a cameo role for his upcoming movie *Get Him to the Greek*.

22 SEPTEMBER 2008

One of the Boys is released in the UK.

30 SEPTEMBER 2008

'Hot n Cold' is released as a single: 'It's about a very real relationship. I was with this boy I really, really cared for and we'd been having a conversation by text or by email and then he'd just disappear. For like three days!'

2 OCTOBER 2008

Three cheerleaders in Texas are suspended from

performing at football games after they twirled their batons to 'I Kissed a Girl' in front of a crowd before a match.

6 NOVEMBER 2008

Katy hosts the MTV Europe Music Awards, held in Liverpool. She opens the show by singing 'I Kissed a Girl', wearing an American football outfit and straddling a gigantic cherry chap-stick in reference to the song's lyrics. During the course of the evening, she manages an incredible *twelve* costume changes as she introduces presenters such as Grace Jones, Bono and Leona Lewis, and watches acts including Take That, Beyoncé, The Killers and Pink perform live. Katy is nominated for two awards, and wins one for Best New Act.

18 NOVEMBER 2008

In an interview, Scarlett Johansson says she is 'flattered' to hear that Katy's song was inspired by her.

8 DECEMBER 2008

Following an alleged media feud with singer Lily Allen, Katy describes herself as a 'fatter version of Amy Winehouse and the skinnier version of Lily Allen'. Lily Allen responds on Capital FM radio by saying that Katy should 'shut up'.

CHRISTMAS 2008

Katy and Travis McCoy travel to Mexico for a holiday but break up on their return.

31 DECEMBER 2008

Travis posts news of the break-up on his blog: 'My lap-top is my new bitch. LOYAL. LISTENS. And NEVER LETS ME DOWN.'

JANUARY 2009

Lily Allen threatens to post Katy's telephone number on Facebook.

13 JANUARY 2009

'Thinking of You' is released. Katy plays an acoustic gig at the Hotel Café in LA and talks about her break-up with Travis. 'It hurts right now.' A video accompanying the song features Katy with her new man but singing about a love who died in the Second World War.

23 JANUARY 2009

The Hello Katy world tour begins in Seattle. Over the next ten months, the tour travels to Asia, Europe, Australia and the USA. Katy performs seventy-nine concerts.

FEBRUARY 2009

In Brazil, teacher Marcio Barros is fired from his job after he used the song 'I Kissed a Girl' in a lesson for twelve-to-fourteen-year-old students and the headmaster decided it promoted homosexuality and alcohol.

FEBRUARY 2009

Newspapers speculate that Katy is dating Benji Madden of the band Good Charlotte.

8 FEBRUARY 2009

Katy performs 'I Kissed a Girl' at the fifty-first Grammy Awards at Los Angeles' Staples Center. To sing the song she is lowered in a vertical banana onto a giant-fruit-covered stage, wearing a corset dress adorned with fruit.

14 FEBRUARY 2009

Katy performs at the Hard Rock Hotel's club Wasted Space in Las Vegas. She is seen later in the evening with Benji Madden at the nightclub Lavo.

15 FEBRUARY 2009

Katy denies reports of a romance with Benji on Twitter: 'Oh kittens! It's two pseudo famous people sitting next to each other . . . doesn't mean we were bumping uglies! You know I don't just do that with anyone!'

18 FEBRUARY 2009

Despite having flu, Katy attends the Brit awards at Earls Court in London. She accepts the award for Best International Female, presented by Lionel Richie, but then has to leave because she feels so ill.

MARCH 2009

Katy tries to apologise about her comments the year

before to Lily Allen in *Heat* magazine: 'I really didn't mean to upset her. What I actually said was that I was a skinnier version of Lily and a fatter version of Amy Winehouse. But Lily is skinny now. She is hot – she looks really good.'

MARCH 2009

Katy tells *Cosmopolitan* magazine that she is not enjoying being single: 'I live this fantastic life, full of these magical things, and at the end of the day all I want to do is pick up my phone and share it with someone.'

25 MARCH 2009

Singer Josh Groban denies press rumours that he and Katy are in a relationship. 'Josh and Katy are very close friends and hang out, but they are not a couple,' says his source.

21 APRIL 2009

'Waking Up in Vegas' is released as a single.

25 APRIL 2009

The *Sun* announces that it has a world exclusive – Katy and Travis are back together: 'The break-up sucked. We're back together now – you're the first person I have told that to,' Travis tells the paper.

16 MAY 2009

Katy attends the Life Ball in Vienna with Travis.

MAY 2009

Katy records acoustic performances of her hits for the TV series *MTV Unplugged*, including re-arranged versions of 'Thinking of You', 'Waking Up in Vegas' and 'I Kissed a Girl', as well as a handful of new songs, the never-before-released 'Brick by Brick' and a cover of Fountain of Wayne's 'Hackensack'.

8 JUNE 2009

Travis is spotted leaving a Las Vegas nightclub with two women. Neither Katy nor Travis make a public comment about it.

9 JUNE 2009

Katy's lawyers allegedly send a letter to fashion designer Katie Perry, asking her to cease using her name on her designs.

9–10 JUNE 2009

Katy plays her biggest London gigs to date at Shepherd's Bush Empire.

11 JUNE 2009

While preparing for that night's show in Brighton, Katy's tour-bus is broken into. Police arrest a burglar before anything is taken. Katy writes on her blog: 'Someone just broke into our bus, they got caught. Luckily all there is is glitter, catsuit outfits, fruit & a box set of *Ab Fab*. Sux fer them.'

JUNE 2009

Beth Ditto criticises Katy and her single 'I Kissed a Girl' in *Attitude* magazine. She described the song as 'a boner dyke anthem for straight girls who like to turn guys on by making out or, like, faking gay'. Katy retaliates by saying she is 'not impressed' by Ditto's comments.

5 JUNE 2009

Katy posts a jokey comment about swine flu on her blog (and a ring she is wearing shaped like a pig) and gets into trouble in the press for it.

19 JUNE 2009

Beth Ditto gives another interview about Katy. 'Honestly, I could care less if Katy Perry's impressed with me. I don't care if she writes a song about kissing a girl, but there are people who kiss girls in their everyday life, and it's not as easy as just kissing a girl and everybody loving you. It'd be really rad to hear her talk about something like that.'

20 JUNE 2009

Katy posts a message on her blog about the fashion designer Katie Perry, saying that she was not intending to sue the other Perry, and that she was only protecting her trademark: 'In the course of securing trademark protection for "Katy Perry" in Australia, it came to the attention of her representatives that Katie Howell, a clothing designer in Australia, had filed an application for trademark protection under a similar name in connection with her own clothing design business. A routine notice letter was sent to Ms Howell, as is customary in trademark practice, alerting her of Ms Perry's intended application. This is a routine trademark application, and I certainly haven't sued anyone.'

11 JULY 2009

Katy plays the festival T in the Park in Scotland. Other acts performing include The Killers, Lady Gaga and Nine Inch Nails.

18 JULY 2009

Australian designer Katie Perry posts on her blog that her problems with Katy had been resolved: 'The battle against my trademark is finished with the withdrawal of opposition from the singer, Katy Perry's lawyers. It is amazing to think that it is all over.'

AUGUST 2009

Katy flies to Los Angeles to be a guest judge on *American Idol*, following the resignation of regular judge Paula Abdul.

19 AUGUST 2009

While being interviewed on the Australian TV show *Sunrise*, Katy's manager – thinking Katy is going to be asked about the lawsuit with Katie Perry – cuts the power to the studio lights to end the interview.

20 AUGUST 2009

After Lady Gaga performs at Glastonbury and photos are circulated on the internet of something between her legs, Katy weighs in on the rumours that the singer is a hermaphrodite: 'Oh please. It's all very calculated, she knows what she's doing. She put something in her knickers, a mini strap on. Bless her if she does have a dick, but I am certain she doesn't.'

22–23 AUGUST 2009

Katy performs at the V Festival at Hylands Park in Essex and Weston Park in Staffordshire with acts including Oasis, Lily Allen, Lady Gaga and The Streets.

30 AUGUST 2009

Katy performs in her home town, at the Santa Barbara Bowl.

6 SEPTEMBER 2009

Katy is spotted wearing a ring on her wedding finger, causing tabloids to speculate that she is now engaged to Travis McCoy.

12 SEPTEMBER 2009

Katy books into the Soho Grand Hotel in New York. Comedian Russell Brand checks into a suite on the same floor.

13 SEPTEMBER 2009

Katy attends the MTV Video Music Awards in New York,

where she is nominated for Best Female Video (for 'Hot n Cold'). Katy sings 'We Will Rock You', accompanied by guitarist Joe Perry, to open the show. She introduces the evening's host, Russell Brand. Kanye West interrupts Taylor Swift's acceptance of an award, causing Katy to tweet: 'F*** you, Kanye. It's like you stepped on a kitten.' Backstage, Katy throws a bottle at Russell Brand's head. The pair are later spotted together at Avenue, where Lady Gaga's after-show party is taking place.

14 SEPTEMBER 2009

Katy and Russell have their first date together. He presents her with a black diamond necklace and a copy of his autobiography.

24 SEPTEMBER 2009

Russell and Katy fly to Thailand and spend a week there together.

6 OCTOBER 2009

According to the tabloids Russell Brand is spotted taking two women back to his London home, amid rumours that he and Katy have already split up.

13 OCTOBER 2009

Katy starts recording her new album, *Teenage Dream*, with producers and writers including Thaddis 'Kuk' Harrell (who worked on Beyoncé's hit 'Single Ladies (Put a Ring on It)' and co-wrote Rihanna's smash hit 'Umbrella'), Rivers Cuomo (of the band Weezer) and

Ryan Tedder (who produced Beyoncé's album *I Am . . . Sasha Fierce*).

NOVEMBER 2009

Katy takes Russell Brand to meet her parents. Her dad, Keith, gives Russell a copy of the religious book he wrote, *The Cry*, while Russell gives Katy's parents a copy of his autobiography *My Booky Wook*.

5 NOVEMBER 2009

Katy is once again asked to present the MTV Europe Awards, held in Berlin. One of the outfits she wears during the evening is a basque in West Ham colours with 'Rusty' (Russell Brand's Twitter name) emblazoned on it.

17 NOVEMBER 2009

Katy releases her *MTV Unplugged* limited-edition CD/DVD, featuring the songs she recorded for MTV in the summer.

28 NOVEMBER 2009

For the final date of the Hello Katy tour, Katy performs at Ischgl in Austria to a packed-out audience. Russell is there with her, along with Katy's parents. ('I really liked her parents, we got on well,' Russell tells the *Daily Mail*. 'But I'm not sure if I want them coming on holiday with us all the time.')

DECEMBER 2009

Russell tells the press: 'I'd love to marry Katy – hopefully it's heading that way and I'm really happy', and journalists begin to speculate as to when he might propose. He puts his London flat on the market and makes an offer on a four-storey home in Los Feliz, Los Angeles.

23 DECEMBER 2009

Russell and Katy are photographed sledging in the snow on Hampstead Heath in London. The next day she flies home to spend Christmas with her parents.

29 DECEMBER 2009

Katy joins Russell on holiday in India, and on 30 December posts a photo on Twitter showing the pair of them standing in front of the Taj Mahal.

31 DECEMBER 2009

Russell Brand proposes to Katy while they are enjoying the New Year celebrations at the Taj Rambagh Palace in India. According to a source at the hotel, they take a horse-and-carriage ride to a garden where they have a romantic meal, and then ride on elephants to watch the New Year's Eve fireworks. Russell then proposes and Katy says yes.

6 JANUARY 2010

Russell's publicist confirms that he and Katy are engaged to be married.

10 JANUARY 2010

The press speculate that Katy is pregnant after she

and Russell are spotted in a children's shoe shop in Hampstead. Katy later denies the rumour on Twitter.

31 JANUARY 2010

Katy attends the fifty-second Grammy Awards in Los Angeles with Russell. She is nominated for Best Female Pop Performance for 'Hot n Cold' but doesn't win.

JANUARY 2010

Katy's appearance as a guest judge on *American Idol* is shown on TV around the world. She falls out with fellow judge Kara DioGuardi as they are deciding who should go through to the next stage of the auditions.

27 MARCH 2010

Katy attends the Nickelodeon Kids' Choice Awards at the UCLA college campus in California. While presenting an award, Katy is 'slimed' (covered in green goo) and slips on the stage while laughing. When Miley Cyrus comes to accept the award, Katy tries to hug her and cover her in the slime but then lets Miley run away.

APRIL 2010

Katy puts the finishing touches to her follow-up album to *One of the Boys*, entitled *Teenage Dream*. She decides it is missing a song and writes 'California Gurls' as a response to the New York-centric hit 'Empire State of Mind'. Snoop Dogg is invited to rap on the song, and he also appears in the video, set in the fictional Candyfornia.

9 APRIL 2010

Katy's friend Rihanna reveals that Katy and Russell's wedding will take place in India later in the year and that she is organising Katy's hen night.

7 MAY 2010

The single 'California Gurls' is released. The song becomes number one on iTunes instantly, sells more than a million downloads in four weeks and is top of *Billboard*'s Hot 100 chart within a month.

15–16 MAY 2010

Katy films the video for 'California Gurls', set in a candy-filled world, and Snoop Dogg guest-stars. The art director is Will Cotton, whose portrait of Katy on a bed of cotton candy features on the cover of her album *Teenage Dream*.

26 MAY 2010

Katy accompanies Russell Brand to the Los Angeles premiere of his new movie *Get Him to the Greek*, even though her cameo appearance in the movie has been cut.

6 JUNE 2010

Katy and Russell attend the MTV Movie Awards. She performs 'California Gurls' on stage with Snoop Dogg, while cameras catch Russell in the audience dancing to her performance.

JUNE 2010

While regular judge Dannii Minogue is on maternity leave, guest judges are asked to appear at the auditions for the 2010 series of *The X Factor*. Katy joins Louis Walsh, Cheryl Cole and Simon Cowell at the auditions in Dublin.

JUNE 2010

Katy makes a comment on Graham Norton's chat-show that leads the press to believe she and Russell Brand are already married. Talking about Russell, she says: 'Life's never dull with him; that's why I married him!'

JULY 2010

Travis McCoy, Katy's ex-boyfriend, releases a solo album with a song about their relationship on it called 'Don't Pretend'. 'In a sense, I felt I'd had my heart ripped out. I'm crying throughout the song. The album is about coming out the other side of something really painful,' he tells the press.

23 JULY 2010

The second single off Katy's new album is released – the title track, 'Teenage Dream'. The video is filmed in Katy's home town of Santa Barbara and features many of her old friends in the background.

5 AUGUST 2010

Representatives from the Beach Boys's record label announce they are going to sue Katy, asking for a co-writing credit and share of the royalties since Snoop Dogg rapped a line from their song 'California Girls' on Katy's 'California Gurls'.

6 AUGUST 2010

Katy posts on Twitter that there is no legal action from the Beach Boys over 'California Gurls'. 'Just to be clear . . . no one is suing anyone,' she writes. 'The press just loves to once again fabricate and exaggerate stories to get hits or sell papers.'

24 AUGUST 2010

Katy's second album as 'Katy Perry', *Teenage Dream*, is released. It features two songs, 'Hummingbird' and 'E.T.', which are supposedly inspired by Russell Brand. The album sells 192,000 copies in the USA in its first week of release.

LATE AUGUST 2010

Katy's appearance on *The X Factor* is broadcast on British TV.

12 SEPTEMBER 2010

Katy appears at the MTV Video Music Awards at the Nokia Theater in Los Angeles. She is nominated for two awards, Best Female Video and Best Pop Video, but loses both to Lady Gaga's 'Bad Romance'. Although Russell Brand isn't with Katy, he is there in spirit – she has his face painted on each of her fingernails.

14 SEPTEMBER 2010

Katy performs a special concert at her old school, Dos Pueblos. She tells the 2,000 students that are gathered there: 'Maybe you don't know, but I went to high school here. I was on this very stage many a lunchtime. I was such a show-off.' She also dedicated a song to Shane Lopes, a boy she'd had a crush on during high school.

19 SEPTEMBER 2010

While waiting to board a flight from Los Angeles to Las Vegas with Katy, Russell Brand is arrested for pushing photographer Marcello Volpe. The photographer is allegedly trying to take a photo up Katy's skirt when Russell shoves him, and the British comedian is arrested on suspicion of battery. Katy tweets: 'If you cross the line & try to put a lens up my dress, my fiancé will do his job & protect me.'

19 SEPTEMBER 2010

Rihanna takes Katy on a hen night to remember in Las Vegas. She arranges for a stretch Hummer car to whisk Katy and twenty-five pals to see Cirque du Soleil in Las Vegas, followed by a boozy trip to a strip club in the city.

23 SEPTEMBER 2010

News breaks that a clip Katy filmed for *Sesame Street* days earlier will not be broadcast on the children's show due to the singer's risqué outfit. When the clip of Katy performing 'Hot n Cold' with red monster puppet Elmo ends up on YouTube, parents complain that her top is too low-cut. *Sesame Street* then releases a statement saying 'we have decided we will not air the segment on the television broadcast of *Sesame Street*, which is aimed at preschoolers'.

26 SEPTEMBER 2010

Russell Brand has his stag night in London. He and friends watch West Ham beat Tottenham Hotspur 1–0, before visiting the Albany pub near Regent's Park and Peter Stringfellow's nightclub, Angels.

27 SEPTEMBER 2010

Katy appears on live TV comedy show *Saturday Night Live* and makes fun of her recent ban from *Sesame Street* by wearing a very tight Elmo T-shirt that is ripped to show off her cleavage.

OCTOBER 2010

A video of an airline crew dancing to a mash-up of Katy's 'California Gurls' and Lady Gaga's 'Let's Dance' becomes an online viral sensation after appearing on YouTube. The staff of Cebu Pacific Airlines in the Philippines co-ordinate their in-flight safety demonstration to the song, with the air hostesses dancing in sync while demonstrating how to put on a life jacket and prepare for an emergency landing. The video scores over six million hits in just five days.

20 OCTOBER 2010

Katy and Russell arrive at Jaipur airport in India, with

Katy sporting a traditional Indian nose ring known as a nath.

21 OCTOBER 2010

Russell's bodyguards attack a group of photographers following Russell, friend David Baddiel and others while on safari at the Ranthambore National Park. The minders later apologise and no arrests are made.

23 OCTOBER 2010

Katy and Russell are married at the Aman-i-Khás hotel. Their publicists release a statement. 'Katy and Russell are overjoyed to confirm that they were pronounced Mr and Mrs Brand on Saturday, October 23. The very private and spiritual ceremony, attended by the couple's closest family and friends, was performed by a Christian minister and long-time friend of the Hudson family. The backdrop was the inspirational and majestic countryside of Northern India.'

26 OCTOBER 2010

The happy couple fly from Jaipur to their honeymoon at the Soneva Fushi resort in the Maldives.

26 OCTOBER 2010

The third single from *Teenage Dream*, 'Firework', is released. It is inspired by a passage in Jack Kerouac's novel *On the Road*. Featuring a video filmed with 250 young fans in Budapest, Katy dedicates it to the It Gets Better Project. 'I am officially dedicating my new video to It Gets Better because everyone has the spark to be a FIREWORK.'

2 NOVEMBER 2010

Reports emerge that Katy may have been bitten by a spider while on honeymoon, and is undergoing medical treatment for it.

3 NOVEMBER 2010

Katy posts a denial about the spider-bite rumour on Twitter. 'I've not been bitten by a spider. I'll file this 1 in the ever growing cabinet of false information that has been at its PEAK as of late . . . '

7 NOVEMBER 2010

Katy performs 'Firework' at the MTV Europe Music Awards in Madrid, and wins the award for Best Video for 'California Gurls'. 'Thank you so much, this is awesome!' she tells the crowd.

11 NOVEMBER 2010

Katy performs in New York at the Victoria's Secret Fashion Show, singing a medley of her hits and also performing 'Firework'.

12 NOVEMBER 2010

Katy launches her first perfume, the fragrance Purr. 'I'm absolutely thrilled to finally introduce me in a bottle!' she says. 'Purr is a natural extension of who I am as a woman. It's a gorgeous blend of all my favourite scents and embodies my style, my tastes and my love for all things incredibly cute. It is an absolutely purrfect perfume that I hope leaves you meowing with delight!'

21 NOVEMBER 2010

Katy attends the American Music Awards in Los Angeles. She is nominated for three awards that she doesn't win, but she wows the crowd with her performance of 'Firework'.

1 DECEMBER 2010

It is announced that Katy has been nominated for four Grammy awards – Album of the Year, Best Female Vocal (for 'Teenage Dream'), Best Pop Collaboration (for 'California Gurls', with Snoop Dogg) and Best Pop Vocal Album for *Teenage Dream*.

5 DECEMBER 2010

Katy appears alongside *Simpsons* puppets in a live-action part of *The Simpsons* episode *The Fight Before Christmas* as bartender Moe's girlfriend.

8 DECEMBER 2010

Katy tells talk-show host Ellen DeGeneres that she is planning to change her name to Mrs Katy Brand.

9 DECEMBER 2010

Katy appears on the cover of US men's magazine *Maxim*, dressed in a leather corset and thigh-high boots.

13 FEBRUARY 2011

The winners of the fifty-third Grammy Awards are announced.

20 FEBRUARY 2011

Katy embarks on the California Dreams tour, beginning in Lisbon. The final date scheduled is 7 November 2011 in Dublin.